j 2717107

DK

My Little
Picture Atlas

A DORLING KINDERSLEY BOOK

LONDON, NEW YORK,
MELBOURNE, MUNICH, and DELHI

Authors Anita Ganeri and Chris Oxlade
Project Senior Editor Ben Morgan
Project Senior Art Editor Janet Allis
Editor Simon Holland
Senior Art Editor Cheryl Telfer
Additional Design Jacqueline Gooden,
Mary Sandberg, Floyd Sayer, Sonia Whillock
Editorial Assistant Fleur Star
Digital Map Illustrator Peter Bull
Publishing Manager Sue Leonard
Managing Art Editor Clare Shedden
Picture Researchers Martin Copeland,
Sean Hunter, Sarah Stewart-Richardson
Production Controller Angela Graef
DTP Designer Emma Hansen-Knarhoi
Jacket Designer Hedi Gutt
Jacket Editor Mariza O'Keeffe

First published in Great Britain in 2003 as DK Picture Atlas
This edition first published in 2006 by
Dorling Kindersley Limited
80 Strand, London WC2R 0RL

Copyright © 2003, 2006 Dorling Kindersley Limited
A Penguin Company

2 4 6 8 10 9 7 5 3 1
DD376 – 10/06

A CIP catalogue record for this book
is available from the British Library.

ISBN 978-1-4053-1900-3

Colour reproduction by Colourscan, Singapore
Printed and bound in Hong Kong

Discover more at
www.dk.com

Contents

Our world

The top of the world

The Americas

Our world

Land covers a third of planet Earth, and water and ice cover the rest. We divide the land into seven main chunks called continents. The sea is divided in five major areas called oceans.

North America

Pacific Ocean

Atlantic Ocean

South America

Inside the Earth

The inside of Earth is made of hot, molten rock that slowly swirls about like thick treacle. We live on a thin, solid crust, a bit like the crust of a pie.

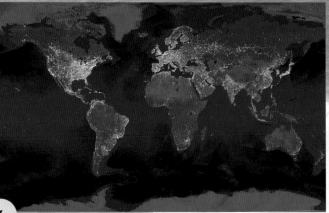

Where people live

This picture of Earth at night was taken by a satellite in space. The bright bits are made by lights on the surface. They show where the world's big cities and towns are.

How long would a trip around the Equator take at walking speed?

E u r o p e

Asia

Pacific
Ocean

Africa

Equator

The Equator is
an imaginary line
around the middle
of the world.

Indian
Ocean

Australia

The Southern Ocean runs all the way around Antarctica.

Southern Ocean

Can you find...

The smallest continent?
The continent of Australia is
also the world's biggest island.

**The most crowded
continent?** About 3,500
million people live in Asia.

Antarctica

Seven continents

North America, South America, Europe,
Asia, Africa, Australia, and Antarctica are
Earth's continents. Sometimes people call
Europe and Asia one continent (Eurasia).

The biggest ocean? The
Pacific Ocean is as big as all
other oceans put together.

About a year (without stopping for a rest).

Maps and atlases

A map is a drawing of the ground that shows where towns, rivers, and other important features lie. An atlas is a book of maps.

Making a flat map of the world is like peeling an orange.

Thin areas need to be stretched to make a full rectangle.

Peeling the Earth
Earth is ball-shaped, so a globe is the best kind of map to show the whole planet. On a flat map, some areas are stretched or squashed.

How to use this book
This atlas is divided into map pages and information pages. The key tells you what the map symbols mean.

Key to maps

- ◉ CAPITAL CITY
- ● State capital
- ● Town
- ▲ Mountain
- ●●● Key feature
- ⌒ Border
- ⌒ State border
- ⌒ River

Compass points show you which way is north, south, east, and west.

Small pictures show the things you might see if you visited the country, from famous buildings to native animals and national sports.

Atlas questions test your general knowledge about different parts of the world. The answer is upside down on the opposite page.

Asia

China and neighbours

Over 1 billion people live in China – that's one-fifth of the world's people. Next door, Mongolia has the fewest people for its size.

Terracotta Army
This army of statues in Xi'an was made more than 2,000 years ago to guard the tomb of Qin Shi Huang, China's first emperor. The statues were rediscovered in 1974.

Chinese opera
Chinese opera has lots of singing, acting, and acrobatics. Make-up is used to show the type of character being played.

Can you find...

The world's tallest mountain? Mount Everest is 8,850 metres (29,035 ft) tall.

The world's most crowded place? Hong Kong has 6,000 people per square kilometre (2,300 per square mile).

China's hottest place? Turpan has recorded temperatures of up to 47°C (117°F).

102 What is the world's second-tallest mountain?

Earth's landscapes
The background patterns on the maps show what the landscape and countryside are like in different parts of the world.

Deciduous forest
Forests of trees that lose their leaves in autumn.

Grassland
Flat, grassy plains with a few trees dotted about.

Coniferous forest
Forests of conifer trees, which are green all year round.

What sort of map shows just countries and their borders?

Types of maps

People use different kinds of maps for different purposes. Road maps help drivers find the way. In cities, people on foot use street maps.

Road maps show routes between towns and cities.

A tube map of London shows underground train stations and the tracks between them.

A street map shows city streets and buildings.

Globes show where the map is on Earth's surface. The featured countries are highlighted in red.

Buttons contain a file of facts about special topics, such as local animals or foods.

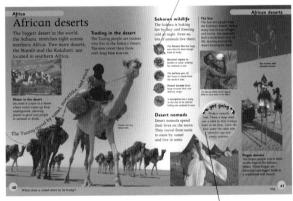

Information pages

After each map are information pages, which are packed with amazing facts about the countries in the map.

Get going circles contain great ideas for projects and experiments you can carry out.

Desert
Dry sand and rock with hardly any plants.

Rainforest
A jungle of tall trees and layers of thick undergrowth.

Snow and ice
High in the mountains and near the poles.

Mountains
Rugged landscape of tall hills and valleys, often snow covered.

Oceans
Seas and oceans cover two-thirds of the Earth.

A political map.

World climates

Near the Earth's poles, it is freezing cold all year round. But near the Equator it is always hot and rainy. We say that the poles and Equator have different climates.

Arctic Circle

Tropic of Cancer

Equator

Tropic of Capricorn

Antarctic Circle

Between the Arctic Circle and the Tropic of Cancer, the climate is temperate.

Between the two tropics, the climate is tropical.

Inside the Arctic and Antarctic circles, the climate is polar.

Climate zones

World maps show horizontal lines that divide Earth into zones with different climates. Tropical zones are always warm and polar zones are always cold. Temperate zones are a mixture of the two, with warm summers and cool winters.

Polar climate

Antarctica has a polar climate. It is always freezing cold, and there are fierce blizzards. Penguins keep warm by growing a thick layer of fat and huddling together.

Conifer forest

In some parts of the temperate zones, winters are long and cold, so conifers are the only trees that survive. Some flowers appear in the short summers.

Emperor penguins

8

What's another name for tropical grassland?

Toucans live in tropical rainforest. They have huge beaks for eating tropical fruits.

Desert

A desert climate is very dry all year round. Deserts can be baking hot in the day but very cold at night.

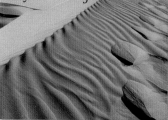

Tropical forest

Places near the Equator are both warm and rainy all year. Dense tropical rainforests grow here.

Tropical grassland

Some tropical places have a dry season and a rainy season every year. Trees are less common here, and the ground is covered with grass.

Deciduous trees change colour as their leaves die in autumn.

Deciduous forest

Warmer parts of the temperate zone are full of trees that shed their leaves in winter. We call them deciduous trees.

Maple leaves

Poison-dart frog

9

SAVANNA.

Seas and oceans

Seas and oceans cover about two-thirds of the world. Beneath the surface they are full of life. Most sea creatures live in habitats near the coast, such as coral reefs. But there is also life far out in the open ocean and on the deep sea floor.

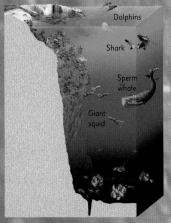

Dolphins

Shark

Sperm whale

Giant squid

Most animals and plants live in the sunlit surface waters near the coast.

Deeper down, the water is cold and gloomy.

No light reaches the deep sea. It is pitch black here.

Ocean waves

Waves are caused by wind blowing across the sea. When they reach shallow water they tumble over and turn into breakers.

Under the sea

Away from the shore, the land slopes steeply into the sea. Some of the seabed is covered in flat plains, but there are also mountains and valleys.

Animals of the deep

Some very strange animals live in the deep sea. The gulper eel lives 7 km (4 miles) down and catches dead creatures as they sink from above. Its mouth is so huge it can swallow animals bigger than itself.

What is the deepest place in the world's oceans?

The open ocean

Out in the open ocean there is less life than near the coast. Occasional shoals of fish are food for big animals, such as dolphins.

Dolphins sometimes drive fish into tight balls before attacking them.

Kelp forests

This seaweed is called giant kelp. It grows from the seabed, making thick forests where fish and other animals live.

Angel fish

Life on the coast

Animals and plants that live on the shore are battered by the waves. They cling to rocks or burrow into sandy beaches.

Tentacle of a sea cucumber (an animal related to a starfish).

Coral reefs

Coral reefs are home to thousands of different sea creatures, including many colourful fish. Reefs grow slowly in shallow tropical seas and are made up of the hard cases of tiny animals (corals).

The Mariana Trench in the Pacific Ocean. It is 11 km (6.9 miles) deep.

The Arctic

At the top of the world is the North Pole, and around this is an area called the Arctic. The Arctic is mostly ocean. In its centre is a gigantic lump of floating ice that never completely melts. Further out are the northern tips of the continents and the huge island of Greenland.

Arctic people

Arctic people live in the icy lands around the Arctic Ocean. The weather is too cold for growing crops, so Arctic people get all their food from animals. They survive by fishing, herding reindeer, and hunting seals and whales.

An imaginary line called the Arctic Circle marks the outer edge of the Arctic region.

Alaska

Prudhoe B

Beaufort Sea

Moose

Queen Elizabeth Islands

Arctic tern

Canada

Ellesmere Island

Ptarmigan

Thule

Polar bear

Greenland

12

Who was the first person to reach the North Pole?

Chukchi Sea

The Arctic tern catches small fish and shrimps by swooping across the surface of the sea.

Seal

Walrus

Arctic Ocean

Laptev Sea

Russian Federation

Arctic Circle

Pole to pole
The Arctic tern spends most of its life flying. It breeds in the Arctic during the northern summer. Then it flies all the way to the Antarctic, where it stays during the southern summer.

The North Pole

Arctic wolf **Norilsk** ●

Kara Sea

Musk ox

Franz Josef Land

Novaya Zemlya

Keeping warm
Arctic animals have to endure bitterly cold weather. Walruses have a layer of blubber (fat) to keep them warm. Polar bears and reindeer have thick coats of fur.

Svalbard

Reindeer

Greenland Sea

Iceberg

Barents Sea

Killer whale

● **Murmansk**

● **Tromsø**

Norwegian Sea

The Arctic

The Arctic is a magical place, but it is also freezing cold and dangerous. For the people and animals that live there, life is very tough indeed.

Arctic travel

Arctic people have to travel across ice, snow, and the sea.

Snowshoes spread your weight to stop your feet sinking into snow.

Skidoos zoom over snow with motorised tracks and a steerable ski.

Kayaks are wooden canoes used by Inuit people for fishing.

Sledges carry heavy loads or people. They are pulled by dogs.

Northern lights

At night, the Arctic sky lights up with shimmering colours called the northern lights. They are caused by particles from space hitting Earth's atmosphere.

Thick fur clothes and fur-lined hoods keep out the cold.

The northern lights look like wavy curtains stretching across the sky.

Rifles are used for hunting and to scare away polar bears.

Inuit hunters

The Inuit people live in Canada and Greenland. They use spears and guns to hunt seals, whales, fish, walruses, and polar bears.

Why is summer in the Arctic unusual?

Polar bear
The world's biggest and most deadly kind of bear is the polar bear, which lives in the Arctic. Polar bears mostly hunt seals, but they occasionally kill people too.

Igloos

Most Inuit people live in modern houses in small towns. On long hunting trips they sleep in igloos – temporary shelters made from blocks of snow.

Icebreakers
In winter the Arctic Ocean freezes solid. Special ships called icebreakers keep channels clear.

Husky dogs

Arctic people use teams of husky dogs to pull sledges. Huskies originally come from Siberia. They are very strong and have thicker fur than most dogs.

Canada and Alaska

Canada is the second-largest country in the world, and Alaska is the largest of all the US states. Despite their huge size, both places have small populations, because much of the land is covered in thick forest or frozen for most of the year.

Ellesmere Island

Queen Elizabeth Islands

Banks Island

Victoria Island

Caribou

Oil drilling

Prudhoe Bay

Musk ox

C

Bering Strait

Huskies pulling sled

Bering Sea

A l a s k a (USA)

Mount McKinley

Great Bear Lake

Yukon

Mackenzie Mountains

Northwest Territories

Yellowknife

Moose

Anchorage

Walrus

Valdez

Whitehorse

Mountie (policeman)

Fur seal

Juneau

British Columbia

Grizzly bear

Salmon

Saskatchewan

Rocky Mountains

Alberta

The Trans-Alaskan Pipeline

The USA's largest oil-drilling area is in Alaska. A huge overground pipeline, 1,270 km (795 miles) long, carries the oil from Prudhoe Bay to the port of Valdez.

Pacific Ocean

Totem pole

Edmonton

Timber

Regi

Vancouver Island

Vancouver

Calgary

Canad

Victoria

Calgary skyline

U S A

What is the tallest mountain in North America, at 6,194 m (20,320 ft) high?

Industries

Here are some of the main industries in the region.

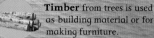

Timber from trees is used as building material or for making furniture.

Oil is used to make fuels like petrol, and chemicals such as plastics.

Wheat is grown in the centre of Canada on prairies, which are huge, flat fields.

Metals such as zinc, aluminium, gold, and silver are mined in Canada.

N E W S

Hooded seal

Baffin Island

Inuit children

Nunavut

Canada goose

Iqaluit

Right whales (whale watching is a popular activity)

Black bear

Newfoundland and Labrador

Newfoundland dog

St. John's

a   n   a   d   a

Hudson Bay

Beluga whale and calf

Mining

Quebec

Gannet

Prince Edward Island

New Brunswick

Charlottetown

Nova Scotia

Halifax

Quebec

Fredericton

Maple leaf

Beaver

Snowboarding

Montreal

CN Tower Toronto

OTTAWA

Manitoba   **Ontario**

Lake Superior

Lake Huron

Lake Michigan

Lake Ontario

Toronto

Lake Erie   Niagara Falls

Atlantic Ocean

Winnipeg

iries

Harbour porpoises

Mount McKinley (Denali).

Canada and Alaska

Magnificent scenery and unspoilt wilderness make Canada and Alaska great places to live. However, the winters are long, dark, and bitterly cold. Most people live in the south, where the weather is mildest.

Alaskan landscape

The ten tallest mountains in the USA are all in Alaska. Mount McKinley (Denali) is the highest. Surrounding these huge mountains are forests and lakes.

Animal life

Despite the chilly weather, Canada, Alaska, and the surrounding sea are home to some spectacular animals.

Husky dogs are used to pull sleds that transport people and materials.

Walruses group together on Arctic beaches or floating sheets of ice.

Moose live in woods close to swamps, lakes, and other watery areas.

Right whales are sometimes hit by ships because they swim slowly.

Fur seals grow to about 2.1 m (7 ft) long. They eat fish and some birds.

Timber industry

Canada's trees can grow to enormous sizes, especially along the rainy west coast. Lumberjacks cut them down for timber (wood), which is used for building houses and making furniture.

What could you put on your pancakes to sweeten them?

Ice hockey

Thanks to the cold winters, Canadians can play ice hockey on outdoor rinks or frozen lakes and ponds. Ice hockey is the world's fastest team sport.

Native peoples

The Kwakiutl and Haida Indians were among the first people to live on Canada's west coast. They carved totem poles to tell stories about their families and traditions.

Totem pole

French Canadians

Europeans started coming to Canada in the 17th century, and many came from France. Today, most French Canadians live in the region called Quebec.

Hotel Chateau Frontenac, Quebec City, Quebec, Canada

Sweet treat

Maple syrup is made from the sap of maple trees. To make it, you drill a hole in a tree, collect the sap that dribbles out, and boil it until it thickens. Sugar maple trees produce the sweetest sap.

CN Tower, Toronto

This is the world's tallest tower (but not the tallest building, since buildings have floors). It is 553 m (1,814 ft) high, which is taller than 300 people standing on each other's heads. A glass lift shoots up the outside to the main deck, which has a revolving restaurant and a scary glass floor.

Maple syrup.

United States of America

The United States of America is an enormous country made up of 50 states. There are mountains, deserts, forests, wetlands, and vast plains in the USA.

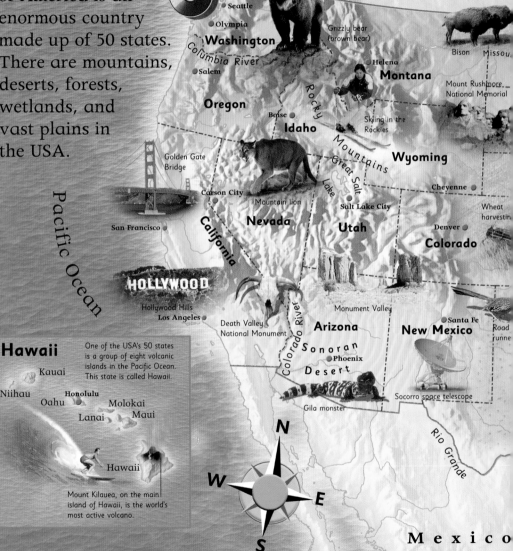

Technology industry

Seattle

Olympia

Washington

Columbia River

Salem

Grizzly bear (brown bear)

Bison   Missou

Oregon

Boise

Idaho

Helena

Montana

Mount Rushmore National Memorial

Skiing in the Rockies

Rocky Mountains

Wyoming

Golden Gate Bridge

Great Salt Lake

Cheyenne

Carson City

Mountain lion

Salt Lake City

Wheat harvestin

San Francisco

California

Nevada

Utah

Denver

Colorado

HOLLYWOOD

Hollywood Hills
Los Angeles

Death Valley National Monument

Colorado River

Monument Valley

Arizona

Sonoran

Santa Fe

New Mexico

Road runne

Phoenix

Desert

Socorro space telescope

Gila monster

Rio Grande

Pacific Ocean

Hawaii

One of the USA's 50 states is a group of eight volcanic islands in the Pacific Ocean. This state is called Hawaii.

Kauai

Niihau

Honolulu

Oahu

Molokai

Lanai

Maui

Hawaii

Mount Kilauea, on the main island of Hawaii, is the world's most active volcano.

N
W   E
S

M e x i c o

20

Which is the only US state not shown on this map?

United States of America

Canada

This map shows 48 of the 50 states of the USA. The other two states are thousands of kilometres away. Alaska is northwest of Canada, and Hawaii is in the middle of the Pacific Ocean.

Lake Superior

Lake Huron

Lake Michigan

Lake Ontario

Lake Erie

Bismarck
North Dakota

Minnesota

Wisconsin

Blueberries

Augusta

Maine

Vermont

New Hampshire

Boston

Pierre

South Dakota

Dairy farming

Michigan

Detroit

New York

Massachusetts

Rhode Island

Connecticut

Statue of Liberty

New York

Iowa

Chicago

Indiana

Ohio

Pennsylvania

Harrisburg

New Jersey

Delaware

Nebraska

Lincoln

Raccoon

Sears Tower, Chicago

American football

WASHINGTON DC

Maryland

West Virginia

Virginia

The Capitol building, Washington, DC

Great Plains

Topeka

Kansas

Missouri

St. Louis

Illinois

American bald eagle

Ohio River

Kentucky

Tennessee

Appalachian Mountains

Raleigh

North Carolina

South Carolina

Atlantic Ocean

Oklahoma City

"Tornado Alley"

Oklahoma

Little Rock

Arkansas

Country music

Mississippi

Mississippi River

Alabama

Atlanta

Georgia

Kennedy Space Center

Dallas

Oil wells

Texas

Paddle steamer

Louisiana

Baton Rouge

New Orleans

Montgomery

Tallahassee

Florida

The Everglades

Miami

Dolphin-watching

Cowboy

Jazz music

Gulf of Mexico

American alligator

Alaska (see page 18).

United States of America

The USA is the world's richest and most powerful country. Many of the people live in huge, modern cities, yet there are still vast areas of unspoilt natural wilderness.

Santa Monica pier and beach, California

The Pacific Coast

The USA's southwest coast has warm, sunny weather and great beaches. Surfers come here for the huge waves, and roller-bladers skate up and down the beachfront.

Visitors climb 354 steps to reach the statue's crown.

New York City

With nearly 8 million inhabitants, New York City is the biggest city in the USA. Its most famous landmark is the Statue of Liberty in the harbour. It is 92 m (305 ft) tall and made of copper.

These towers of rock are

What is the hottest place in the USA?

Hawaii

The Hawaiian islands are the tops of volcanoes in the Pacific Ocean. Mount Kilauea has been erupting for years. Its lava flows into the sea and makes huge clouds of steam.

The Mississippi River

The Mississippi is North America's longest river. Barges carry cargos like oil, coal, and steel along it. Here the Mississippi is flowing past the Gateway Arch in St Louis, Missouri.

American alligator

Swamps and alligators

There are huge grassy swamps called the Everglades in the state of Florida. The swamps are home to all sorts of wild animals, including alligators, panthers, and turtles.

the crumbling remains of ancient mountains.

Deserts and canyons

Southwestern USA is hot and dry. There are spectacular rocky towers called mesas, cactus-filled deserts, and deep canyons.

get going

Make an American flag like the one in the back of this book. Draw 7 red stripes on a sheet of paper, but leave a corner blank. Colour the corner blue and stick 50 small small white stars on it.

Death Valley, California.

The Capitol building, Washington, DC.

Life in the USA

The USA is one of the world's most diverse countries. Most Americans are descended from people who moved here from other countries.

Capitol in the capital
Washington, DC, is the capital of the USA and home of the US government. Senators and congressmen meet in the Capitol building to make laws.

Musical roots
Modern rock and pop music grew from jazz and blues, which were invented by African Americans about 100 years ago.

The city of New Orleans is the home of jazz.

Independence Day
The USA became an independent country on 4 July 1776. The Fourth of July is a holiday called Independence Day. There are parties and big parades through the streets.

Independence Day parade

Where is Hollywood?

American food

America's food is as varied as its people.

Hamburgers are not made from ham, but from ground beef.

Clam chowder is seafood soup from New England, northeast USA.

Tex-Mex is a mixture of flavours from Texas and Mexico.

Gumbo is a spicy soup from Louisiana, made with meat and seafood.

American Indians

American Indians have lived in the USA for thousands of years. Today, about one in 100 Americans is American Indian.

These girls are wearing the traditional clothes of Navajo Indians. The Navajo live in Arizona and New Mexico.

American football

American football

The top spectator sport in the USA is American football. More than 40 million people a year go to watch games, often in big stadiums.

Rodeo rider on a bull

Rodeo rider

People visit rodeos to watch cowboys show off their riding skills. The cowboy tries to stay on a bucking horse or bull as long as he can.

The Oscar award is given for excellence in making films.

© A.M.P.A.S.®

Film industry

American films are watched all over the world. Hollywood is the home of the film industry.

In the city of Los Angeles, California.

N W E S

Tijuana

Sonoran Desert

USA

Prickly pear cactus

Gulf of California

Baja California

Rio Grande River

Cattle

Sierra Madre Occidental

Monarch butterflies

Sierra Madre Oriental

Armadillo

Monterrey

Boojum tree

Los Mochis

Mariachi

Atlante statue at Tula

Gulf of Mexico

La Paz

Brown pelican

Grey whale

Agave

M e x i c o

Pacific Ocean

Guadalajara

Catedral Metropolitana

MEXICO CITY

Veracruz

Acapulco

Mexico and Central America

Mexico and Central America form a natural bridge linking the USA to South America. The north of Mexico is dry and dusty. As you travel south, the weather gets rainier and the land becomes greener, with lush rainforests covering mountains and volcanoes.

Did you know?

Coffee beans and bananas are Costa Rica's most important crops.

Chocolate was first made in Mexico, from the seeds of the cacao tree.

Sugar cane from Central America and the Caribbean is used to make sugar.

How do spider monkeys use their tails?

West Indies
To the east of Central America is a chain of tropical islands called the West Indies. The weather here is warm all year, but hurricanes can strike in summer.

Bahamas

HAVANA
Cuba

Palm tree

Pineapples

Atlantic Ocean

Dominican Republic

Haiti
PORT-AU-PRINCE

SANTO DOMINGO

SAN JUAN
Puerto Rico

Lesser Antilles

Greater Antilles

Jamaica
KINGSTON

Dominica

St Lucia

Frigate

Caribbean Sea

Yacht

Barbados

PORT-OF-SPAIN
Trinidad and Tobago

Flamingos

Chichén Itzá

Coral reef

Olmec head

Macaw

Green turtle

Belize
● BELMOPAN

Grapefruit

Panama Canal
The man-made Panama Canal links the Atlantic and Pacific Oceans. About 12,000 ships pass through it every year, making it one of the world's busiest waterways.

Shrimp

Guatemala **Honduras**

TEGUCIGALPA

GUATEMALA CITY

El Salvador
SAN SALVADOR

Bananas

Nicaragua
MANAGUA ● Lake Nicaragua

get going
Cut the leafy top off a pineapple and plant it in a pot of soil. If you keep it in a greenhouse, it will grow into a pineapple plant.

Costa Rica
SAN JOSÉ

Panama Canal

Spider monkey

Panama
PANAMA CITY

Toucan

As hooks to hang from branches.

Mexico and Central America

Mexico and Central America are a melting pot of bustling cities, ancient ruins, and steamy jungles. Most of the people speak Spanish.

Aztecs and Mayas

Hundreds of years ago, the Aztec and Maya peoples built fabulous cities in the jungles and mountains. Their crumbling ruins survive to this day.

This man is dressed as an Aztec warrior. The Aztecs used to sacrifice their enemies and rip their hearts out.

Around 1,000 years ago, this pyramid was the centre of a huge Mayan city called Chichén Itzá.

What is the name for a Mexican pancake, made from maize and flour?

Agriculture

Central America is warm and wet – perfect weather for tropical crops like bananas, maize, avocados, and peppers. Farmers sell their crops in the busy local markets.

Mexico City

Mexico's capital was built on the ruins of an ancient Aztec city. It is now one of the world's biggest cities, with 20 million people.

Tacos and tortillas

Mexicans like spicy food flavoured with chillis. These are tacos – fried pancakes full of meat and vegetables. The pancakes are called tortillas.

Caribbean paradise

The sunny islands of the Caribbean attract tourists by the million. They come to laze on beautiful, sandy beaches, swim in the warm sea, and snorkel over coral reefs.

get going

Get a slice of bread and roll it out flat using a rolling pin. Now add your favourite filling and roll the bread around it. You've just made a Mexican enchilada!

A tortilla (pronounced "tor-teeya").

29

South America

A vast chain of mountains runs the length of this continent. On its western side is the world's driest desert. On the east is the biggest rainforest.

Equator walkabout

The Equator is an imaginary line around Earth's middle. It would take you a month to walk across just the South American part of it!

Bananas

Brazil nuts

Belem

Copybara

Brazil

CAYENNE

PARAMARIBO

French Guiana

GEORGETOWN

Suriname

Guyana

CARACAS

Venezuela

Orinoco

Angel Falls

Cartagena

Agrias butterfly

BOGOTÁ

Colombia

QUITO

Ecuador

Equator

Amazon Rainforest

Manaus

River Amazon

Jaguar

Machu Picchu

Peru

Condor

Andes Mountains

LIMA

Arequipa

Lake Titicaca

LA PAZ

Bolivia

Pacific Ocean

What is the highest mountain in the Andes?

Oil rig

• Salvador

football

●BRASÍLIA

São Paulo   ● Rio de Janeiro

Sugar Loaf Mountain

Atlantic Ocean

Green turtle

Can you find...

The world's highest capital?
La Paz, Bolivia, is 3,632 m (11,916 ft) above sea level.

The world's highest waterfall?
Angel Falls in Venezuela measures 979 m (3,212 ft) from top to bottom.

The world's driest town?
Arica in Chile's Atacama Desert has an annual rainfall of zero!

Gaucho

Paraguay

ASUNCIÓN

Bolivian Indian

Llama

Argentina

Uruguay

●MONTEVIDEO

Pampas grass

BUENOS AIRES

Pampas

● Bahía Blanca

Cape Horn

The southern tip of South America is called Cape Horn. The seas around it are so stormy that hundreds of ships have been shipwrecked there.

Magellan penguins

Chile

Atacama Desert

Andes Mountains

Aconcagua

Valparaíso ● ● SANTIAGO

Sheep farming

Patagonia

Mackerel

Cape Horn

Aconcagua, which is 6,960 m (22,834 ft) high.

South America

One third of South America is covered by a huge jungle called the Amazon rainforest. To the east and south of the rainforest are rich grasslands, enormous cattle ranches, and South America's biggest cities.

Scarlet macaw

Forest life

Native people have lived in the Amazon jungle for thousands of years. They survive by hunting and gathering wild food, without harming the forest.

Yanomami village in the Amazon rainforest.

Deadly animals

The Amazon rainforest is home to all sorts of dangerous creatures.

Forest people use **poison-dart frogs** to make deadly poison for arrows.

The **jaguar** is a very secretive cat. It is a good swimmer and climber.

Piranhas are vicious fish with very sharp teeth. They hunt in packs.

The **boa constrictor** kills animals by squeezing them to death.

Gauchos

Argentinian gauchos are like American cowboys. They work on vast ranches in the pampas grasslands of Argentina, where they look after cattle and horses.

Dug-out canoe on the Amazon

What language do most Brazilians speak?

Highest waterfall

Angel Falls in Venezuela is the world's highest waterfall. The water tumbles off a flat-topped mountain and plunges 980 m (3,215 ft) to the ground. That's three times the height of New York's Empire State Building.

Granadillas grow on jungle vines.

Forest fruits

The granadilla (a kind of passion fruit) is one of many exotic fruits that grow in tropical parts of South America.

Rio de Janeiro

A statue of Christ towers over Rio de Janeiro, Brazil's second-largest city. In the bay is the dome-shaped Sugar Loaf Mountain.

Carnival

Every year, Rio de Janeiro holds a spectacular carnival that lasts four days. People dress up in brilliant costumes and dance through the streets, blowing whistles and singing.

Life in the Andes

The Andes stretch all the way down South America, forming the world's longest mountain range. The people and animals that live in the Andes are used to the cold, thin air.

Condor
The Andean condor is a huge bird of prey. In flight, its wings measure 3 m (10 ft) from tip to tip.

Machu Picchu

High in the Andes in Peru are the ruins of an ancient city called Machu Picchu. The city was built about 500 years ago by people called Incas.

Llamas
A llama is like a tall sheep. People in the Andes keep llamas for their warm wool, their milk and meat, and for carrying cargo.

What is the most southerly city in the world?

Atacama Desert
The Atacama is the largest desert in South America. It is officially the driest place on Earth because it hardly ever rains here.

Valparaíso
Sandwiched between the mountains and the coast is Valparaíso, one of Chile's biggest cities. It is Chile's main port.

get going
Make some panpipes. Join a row of ten straws with sticky tape. Cut the bottoms of the straws at an angle. Blow across the straws to play the pipes.

Pan pipes
The pan pipes are a traditional Andean musical instrument. They are made from hollow reeds or bamboo.

Mountain people
Many people who live in the Andes are South American Indians. Their families have lived in the Andes for hundreds of years.

People from the Andean city of Cuzco, Peru, wear very colourful clothes.

Sailing on top of the world
At 3,800 metres (12,450 ft) high, Lake Titicaca is the highest lake in the world that ships can sail on. Local people fish the lake in boats made from reeds.

Punta Arenas, Chile.

Africa

Africa is a vast, sun-baked continent, famous for its amazing wildlife. In the north and south are hot deserts. Between the deserts are swampy rainforests and grasslands full of wild animals.

N · E · S · W

Asia

Red Sea

Eritrea
ASMARA

Djibouti

Horn of Africa

ADDIS ABABA

Ethiopia

Great Rift Valley

KHARTOUM

Nubian Desert

Aswan

Sudan

Suez Canal

River Nile

CAIRO

Egypt

Pyramids

Nile felucca boat

Mediterranean Sea

Gulf of Sirte

TRIPOLI

Al 'Aziziyah

Libya

Cheetah

Central African Rep.

BANGUI

Hippopotamus

NDJAMENA

Lake Chad

Chad

TUNIS

Tunisia

Bedouin weaver

Ahaggar Mountains

Erg Tifernine

Niger

Sahel

Cameroon

ALGIERS

Algeria

Sahara Desert

Ostriches

NIAMEY

ABUJA

Nigeria

Cocoa bean

Ait Benhaddou mud fortress, Morocco

Atlas Mountains

Tuareg nomads

Mali

River Niger

Burkina

Benin
Togo

Ghana

RABAT

Morocco

BAMAKO

Bambara village

Ivory Coast

Liberia

Sierra Leone

Guinea

Guinea-Bissau

LAAYOUNE

Western Sahara

Mauritania

NOUAKCHOTT

Peanuts

Senegal
DAKAR

Gambia

Atlantic Ocean

How long is Africa from north to south?

MOGADISHU

Dhow sailing boat

Lemur

ANTANANARIVO

Chameleon

Madagascar

Madagascar

The island of Madagascar is home to tree-dwelling animals called lemurs. They have faces like cats but bodies like monkeys.

Mozambique Channel

Uganda

Tea

Kenya

KAMPALA

NAIROBI

Mount Kilimanjaro

Lake
Victoria

Rwanda

Burundi

Serengeti

DODOMA

Tanzania

Elephant

Malawi

Great Rift Valley

Mozambique

Masai herder

LUSAKA

Zambezi River

Zimbabwe

MAPUTO

Swaziland

PRETORIA

Lowland
gorilla

Diamond mine

KINSHASA

Dem. Rep.
of Congo

Zambia

Angola

Zebra

Victoria Falls

Kalahari Desert

Botswana

Ndeble
house

Lesotho

South Africa

Cape of Good Hope

Congo River

Gabon

LUANDA

Oil rig

Hornbill

Giraffe

WINDHOEK

Namibia

Namib Desert

Tin and
copper
mining

Springbok

Cape Town

Atlantic Ocean

Equatorial Guinea

Can you find...

The highest point in Africa?
Mount Kilimanjaro in Tanzania is 5,895 m (19,341 ft) tall.

One of the world's highest sand dunes? Erg Tifernine in the Sahara is 400 m (1,300 ft) tall.

The hottest place on Earth?
Al 'Aziziyah, in Libya, has had temperatures of 58°C (136.4°F).

The Suez Canal

This canal is a man-made waterway that runs from the Red Sea to the Mediterranean. It provides a short cut for ships travelling from Europe to Asia.

Savanna wildlife

Much of Africa is covered by a type of grassland called savanna. Huge herds of grazing animals live on the savanna, as well as lions, hyenas, and cheetahs.

Life in Africa

There are about 50 countries in Africa, but hundreds of different peoples and more than 1,000 languages. Most African people are farmers who live in the countryside. In recent times, many people have moved into cities.

Villagers in Ghana carrying water

Mosquitoes spread malaria when they bite people.

Masai people often wear lots of red to scare off lions.

Health and disease

Poor health is a problem in some parts of Africa. Many Africans have to walk for hours every day to fetch clean water. Diseases such as malaria are common.

Masai necklaces

The Masai people of east Africa lead a traditional way of life, herding their cows across the land. Masai women wear colourful beaded necklaces to show off how rich they are.

What is the world's largest continent?

Living in the city
One out of every five Africans lives in bustling cities, such as Cape Town. People move to the cities to find work and a better life.

Drummers from Ghana

African music
African people love music and dancing. These musicians come from Ghana in west Africa. Their drums are made from animal skins pulled tight by strings.

Safaris save animals
Tourists come to Africa's savanna (grassland) to see the wildlife. The money the tourists spend helps to save rare animals, such as rhinos.

Rainforest life
In the rainforests of central Africa, some people get their food from the wild. They travel through the forest, hunting animals and gathering fruit.

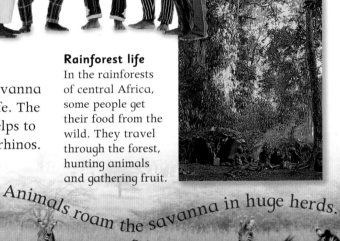

Animals roam the savanna in huge herds.

Asia. Africa is the second largest.

African deserts

The biggest desert in the world, the Sahara, stretches right across northern Africa. Two more deserts, the Namib and the Kalahari, are located in southern Africa.

Trading in the desert

The Tuareg people are traders who live in the Sahara Desert. The men cover their faces with long blue scarves.

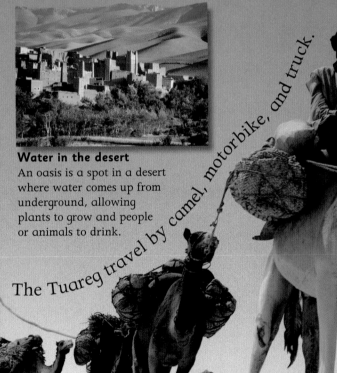

Water in the desert

An oasis is a spot in a desert where water comes up from underground, allowing plants to grow and people or animals to drink.

The Tuareg travel by camel, motorbike, and truck.

Camels can carry heavy loads.

What does a camel store in its hump?

Saharan wildlife

The Sahara is baking hot by day and freezing cold at night. Even so, lots of animals live there.

 The **fennec fox** has huge ears that let heat escape from its body.

 Horned vipers lie hidden in sand, looking for animals to eat.

 The **jerboa** gets all the water it needs from the seeds it eats.

 Desert locusts form huge swarms that can destroy crops.

 A **scorpion** has a sting at the end of its tail for killing the animals it eats.

Desert nomads

Desert nomads spend their lives on the move. They travel from oasis to oasis by camel and live in tents.

The San

The San are people from the Kalahari Desert. Today many San live in villages and towns, but some still lead a traditional way of life, moving around the desert hunting for food.

San hunters with poisoned arrows

The San use hollow ostrich eggs as flasks to carry water in the desert.

get going

Make a nomad's tent. Throw a large sheet over a table so that it hangs down to the floor. Cover the floor under the table with colourful rugs and comfy cushions.

Dogon dancers

The Dogon people live in Mali on the edge of the Sahara Desert. These Dogon are imitating long-legged birds in a traditional stilt dance.

The River Nile

Life in northeast Africa would be impossible without the Nile, the world's longest river. It flows right across the Sahara Desert, providing vital water and a highway for boats.

Lake Victoria is the main source of the Nile.

The route of the Nile
The Nile begins in Uganda and flows 6,700 km (4,200 miles) north, passing through Sudan and Egypt.

Aswan dams
At Aswan in Egypt, two huge dams have been built to store water and to generate electricity.

Sailing the Nile

In Egypt, people sail up and down the Nile on wooden boats called feluccas. It hardly ever rains in Egypt, so the crew sleep on the open deck at night.

Abu Simbel
The Abu Simbel temples were built by the ancient Egyptians. Engineers moved them to save them from being drowned when the Aswan High Dam was built.

Who was buried in Egypt's biggest pyramid?

City on the Nile

Cairo is the capital of Egypt and the biggest city in Africa. Around 10 million people live in Cairo, many of them in crowded slums.

Nile Delta from space

Nile Delta

The Nile dumps lots of silt at its mouth, forming a muddy area called a delta. Crops grow especially well here.

Nile crops

These crops grow on the banks of the Nile.

Wheat is grown for making flour, which is used in bread-making.

Dates are delicious fruits. Date tree leaves are woven into baskets.

Fibres from **cotton seeds** are used to make yarn and fabrics.

The Pyramids

Huge pyramids stand in the desert near Cairo. The pyramids were built thousands of years ago as tombs for ancient kings called pharaohs.

The Sphinx has a lion's body and a man's head.

Egyptian farmers use donkeys to pull carts.

Farming on the Nile

Farmers take water from the Nile to irrigate their fields. There is a narrow strip of farmland on each bank of the river. The Sahara Desert lies beyond the fields.

Pharaoh Khufu (Cheops).

43

Russian Federation

Arctic Ocean

North Cape

Reindeer

Wolf

Sauna

Paper mill

River Kemijoki

Oulu

Gulf of Bothnia

Lapland

Mining

Tromso

Grey seal

Sweden

Kjolen Mountains

Fishing trawler

Lynx

Vesterfjorden

Puffin

Wolverine

Norwegian Sea

Atlantic Ocean

Scandinavia

The northernmost part of Europe is Scandinavia – a region of dense pine forests, snowy mountains, and craggy coastlines.

Iceland

Iceland is a volcanic island in the far north Atlantic Ocean. It has hundreds of hot springs and geysers.

Greenland Sea

Church of Hallingrimur

Vatnajökull (Ice sheet)

Geyser

REYKJAVÍK

Which Scandinavian warriors raided Europe in 800–1050 AD?

The Øresund Bridge

The Øresund Bridge links Copenhagen in Denmark to Malmö in Sweden. There are three parts to the bridge — an underground tunnel, an artificial island, and a bridge over the sea. Together, they are 16 km (10 miles) long.

Faeroe Islands

These islands are part of Denmark. They lie halfway between Iceland and Scotland.

Torshavn

Finland

Rainbow trout

Cathedral, Helsinki

HELSINKI

Gulf of Finland

Åland Islands

STOCKHOLM

Golden eagle

Cross-country skiing

City Hall, Stockholm

Rune stone

Gotland

Öland

Baltic Sea

Swedish glass

Bornholm

N E S W

Norway

Stave church

Mount Galdhøppigen 2,469 m (8,100 ft)

OSLO

Lake Vänern

Lake Vättern

Gothenburg

COPENHAGEN

Malmö

Little Mermaid statue, Copenhagen

Sculptures in Vigeland Park, Oslo

Oslo Fjord

Denmark

Dairy farming

Pig farming

Lego

Nord Fjord

Sogne Fjord

Bergen

Hardanger Fjord

Boks Fjord

Stavanger

North Sea

Herring

Scandinavia

Ski jumper, Norway

Scandinavians enjoy a spectacular landscape and a high standard of living. But they also have to cope with long, dark, icy winters.

Pine forests cover much of Scandinavia.

Winter sports
Winter sports are very popular in Scandinavia. Many top ski jumpers come from this region.

All the houses in Legoland are built from Lego.

Legoland
The Legoland theme park in Denmark is built from 50 million Lego™ bricks. Lego was invented in Denmark in 1949.

Viking ships
The Vikings lived in Scandinavia 1,000 years ago. They raided other countries in longships like this one.

Timber industry
In Scandinavia, millions of trees are grown for their wood. The timber is made into houses, furniture, and paper.

What is a Finnish steam room called?

Wildlife

The animals that live in Scandinavia are well adapted to the cold.

Arctic foxes have thick white fur for warmth and camouflage in the snow.

The **lynx** is a type of cat from the forests of Norway and Sweden.

Puffins are small seabirds. They swim underwater to catch fish.

Elks are large deer. Their huge antlers can be 2 metres (6.5 ft) wide.

Naturally hot
Iceland has many volcanoes, geysers, and hot springs. The water in this lake is heated by hot rocks deep underground.

Norwegian fjords

Hundreds of narrow valleys cut into the coast of Norway. They are called fjords. Ships can shelter here from bad weather.

Lapland

The north of Scandinavia is called Lapland. The people who live there are Lapps or Sami. Some Lapps herd reindeer for their fur, meat, and milk.

A sauna.

Shetland
Islands

Orkney
Islands

Thurso

Outer Hebrides

Skye

Red deer

Highland cow

Mull

Giant's
Causeway

Loch Ness
Monster

Aberdeen

Grampian
Mountains

Ben Nevis
1,343 m (4,406 ft)

Scotland

River Forth

Glasgow

Bagpiper

Edinburgh

Edinburgh
Castle

North Sea

Angel of the North

Newcastle upon Tyne

**Northern
Ireland**

UK and Ireland

The United Kingdom is made up of
England, Scotland, Wales, and Northern
Ireland. Ireland is a separate country.
Most of the people in the UK and Ireland
speak English as their main language.

The Royal Family

England and Scotland had
separate royal families until
1603, when they joined together
to form the United Kingdom.
Queen Elizabeth II is the
current Head of State.

What is the name of the Queen's official residence in London?

North Sea oil rig

Yacht

N o r f o l k B r o a d s

Dover

Eurotunnel to France

Cambridge

Middlesbrough

Kingston upon Hull

Big Ben

E n g l a n d

LONDON

Brighton

Royal Pavillion

Pennines

L a k e D i s t r i c t

Manchester

Blackpool Tower

Football

Birmingham

Oxford

River Thames

Isle of Wight

Portland Bill lighthouse

Stonehenge

E n g l i s h   C h a n n e l

F r a n c e

Liverpool

S n o w d o n i a

Crufts dog show

River Severn

Douglas

Isle of Man

Irish Sea

C a m b r i a n M o u n t a i n s

W a l e s

Cardiff

E x m o o r

D a r t m o o r

Exeter

Eden Project

DUBLIN

Sheep

Surfing

The Eden Project, Cornwall
These giant greenhouses are home to lots of plants from different areas of the world. People can visit here to learn how important nature is to the future of the planet.

I r e l a n d

Blarney Castle

Galway

Cork

Isles of Scilly

L a n d ' s   E n d

Cathedral

Jaunting car

N
E
S
W

UK and Ireland

The islands that make up the UK and Ireland are called the British Isles. The British Isles are famous for their history, traditions, and for their green – though rainy – countryside.

The London Eye

London is the capital of the UK and the site of the London Eye – a gigantic ferris wheel that gives tourists a stunning view over the city.

Passengers ride the Eye in glass capsules.

Fish and chips

British food has been influenced by many cultures, but the traditional meal of fried fish and chips is still a popular dish.

Stately home

Windsor Castle near London is one of the Queen's homes. It is the largest occupied castle in the world and has around 1,000 rooms. Certain parts of the castle are open to tourists.

Grenadier guards wear a tall hat made from the fur of Canadian black bears.

The Queen's private army of guards are called beefeaters.

Which Welsh village has the longest place name in Europe?

Down the pub

Nearly every town and village in the UK and Ireland boasts at least one pub, where people go to relax and meet their friends. Irish pubs serve a famous type of beer called Guinness, which is jet black and very frothy.

A pint of Guinness

British sports

Sports invented in Britain are now played all over the world.

 Cricket is played in summer. Some matches last for five days.

 Football is the world's most popular sport, watched by billions.

 Rugby is played with an oval ball that the players pick up and run with.

Scottish lakes are called lochs.

Rocky coast

Rugged cliffs and strange rock formations dot the north coast of Northern Ireland. The wobbly Carrick-a-rede Rope Bridge leads to a tiny island.

Highland cow

Scottish highlands

Northern Scotland has some of the UK's quietest countryside, with miles of rolling mountains and glassy lakes. There are few people here, apart from farmers and hikers.

Football and rugby

Football and rugby matches attract huge crowds of fans in the UK. English and Scottish people are great football fans. Welsh people also like rugby.

The Low Countries

Belgium, the Netherlands, and Luxembourg are called the Low Countries because they are so flat. They are also sometimes called Benelux – the first letters of BElgium, NEtherlands and LUxembourg.

Germany

Netherlands

Avocet

Cattle

Cyclist

Horse

Ice skating

West Frisian Islands

Waddenzee

River Rhine

Arnhem

Flevoland

IJsselmeer

Windmills

Clogs

Eindhoven

Tern

Cheese porters

AMSTERDAM

Tulips

Barge

Antwerp Cathedral

North Sea

Rotterdam

The Hague

Cubic Houses

Fishing

Herring

Dams to stop floods from sea

Bruges Town Hall

Bruges

Ostend

N E S W

What is another name for the Netherlands?

Did you know..?

Brussels is the capital of Europe. It is the centre of the European Union and home of the European Parliament.

900 windmills along the Netherlands' coast help to keep the land drained.

Wooden clogs were first invented by Dutch workmen 600 years ago.

Lace making

BRUSSELS

Chocolates

The Atomium

Belgium

Crystal

Charleroi

Liège

River Meuse

Beer

Deer

A r d e n n e s   F o r e s t

Wild boar

Vianden castle

Luxembourg

LUXEMBOURG

France

Amsterdam

The tall houses lining the canals of Amsterdam were built by rich spice merchants hundreds of years ago. Each one is unique, and many are crooked because they are built on marshy land.

The Low Countries

Large parts of the Low Countries used to be underwater, but people worked out how to turn the shallow sea into farmland. The area is now famous for growing flowers.

Amsterdam

People sometimes call Amsterdam "the Venice of the north" because the city is riddled with canals and full of beautiful old houses. Cycling is popular here as there are few cars in the town centre and no hills.

The Dutch make 3 million pairs of clogs (wooden shoes) each year. Farmers used to wear shoes like this for working in boggy fields.

get going

Make a windmill. Cut a cross from paper 10 cm across. Twist each arm slightly the same way. Pin the centre to a pencil and blow on the back to make it spin.

Cheese market

On Fridays, Dutch cheese-makers hold a traditional market in the town of Alkmaar to sell huge wheels of cheese. The most popular cheeses are Edam, which is covered with red wax, and Gouda.

How much of the Netherlands used to be under the sea?

The medieval castle at
Vianden, Luxembourg

Dutch master

Vincent van Gogh
(1853–90) was a
brilliant, but mad,
Dutch artist who
cut off his own
ear. He painted
this self-portrait
in 1889.

Luxembourg

Luxembourg is a tiny, but rich,
country with beautiful scenery
and spectacular castles. The
people speak a language called
Letzebuergesch.

Windmills

The Dutch once used
windmills to pump water
out of low land, but now
they mostly use electric
pumps. Dykes (earth
banks) stop the water
flooding back in.

The Atomium

This strange building in
Brussels is a model of nine
iron atoms, enlarged 165
billion times. Visitors can go
inside six of the "atoms",
which are joined
by escalators.

France

France is the biggest country in western Europe. Its capital is the city of Paris, site of the Eiffel Tower. France is famous for its scenic countryside, which is dotted with sleepy villages and fairytale castles called châteaux.

English Channel

Mont St-Michel   Bayeux Tapestry

Breton woman

Rennes   Le Mans race track

Le Mans

Standing Stones (Carnac)

Mont St-Michel

A towering abbey sits on the island of Mont St-Michel off the north coast of France. At low tide, people can walk across the sand to get to Mont St-Michel.

Mackerel

Beef cattle

Brandy

Atlantic Ocean

Bordeaux

Bay of Biscay

Wine

Cave Paintings at Lascaux

Biarritz

Aeroplane manufacturing   Toulous

Pyrenees Mountains

56

Where in France would you find pink flamingos and wild horses?

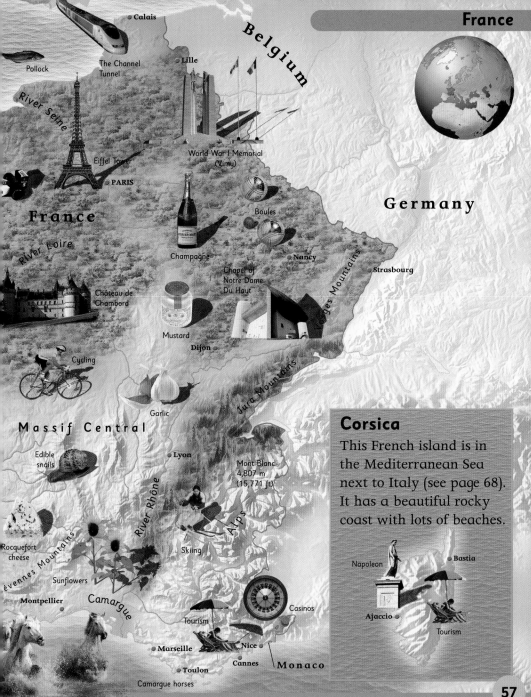

Calais

The Channel Tunnel

Pollock

River Seine

Belgium

Lille

World War I Memorial (Vimy)

Eiffel Tower

PARIS

France

Germany

River Loire

Boules

Champagne

Nancy

Strasbourg

Chapel of Notre Dame Du Haut

Château de Chambord

Vosges Mountains

Mustard

Dijon

Cycling

Garlic

Jura Mountains

Massif Central

Edible snails

Lyon

Mont Blanc
4,807 m
(15,771 ft)

River Rhône

Corsica

This French island is in the Mediterranean Sea next to Italy (see page 68). It has a beautiful rocky coast with lots of beaches.

Rocquefort cheese

Skiing

Alps

Napoleon

Bastia

Sunflowers

Montpellier

Camargue

Ajaccio

Cévennes Mountains

Tourism

Casinos

Tourism

Marseille

Nice

Monaco

Toulon

Cannes

Camargue horses

The marshes of the Camargue.

57

France

Perfumes, bread, edible snails, and champagne are a few of the things that France is famous for. Millions of tourists visit Paris each year to see its beautiful buildings, parks and museums.

Café culture
French people love to sit in cafés and watch the world go by. This café is on a wide avenue called the Champs-Élysées.

A famous landmark

The Eiffel Tower is the most famous landmark in France. It is 300 metres (984 feet) high and was built in 1889. Tourists can go up to the top platform.

Visitors can walk up to the first and second floors.

get going
Fields of sunflowers are a common sight in France. Grow your own sunflower by planting a seed in a pot of soil in spring. Water it every week and it will be taller than you by summer.

How many people visit the Eiffel Tower each year?

Food and wine

French restaurants serve some of the best food in the world. France is also famous for making wine.

Snails are a French delicacy. They are cooked in their shells with garlic.

Croissants are made from fluffy pastry. People eat them for breakfast.

Champagne is a fizzy white wine. It is made in an area called Champagne.

Luxury houses

A large French country house is called a château. This one is Château d'Azay-le-Rideau. It was built 500 years ago and is surrounded by a lake.

Fast trains

The French TGV is the fastest express train in the world. It speeds along its special track at 300 km (190 miles) per hour.

Cheese making

France makes 400 kinds of cheese, many of which are eaten all over the world. This cheese-maker taps the cheese to check if it has any holes.

Cyclists on the Tour de France, a three-week race.

About 200 cyclists enter the race.

Cycle racing

The Tour de France is the world's greatest cycle race and lasts for thousands of miles. French people stop work or school to watch the cyclists as they ride through town.

Many French farmers grow grapes for making wine.

About 6 million.

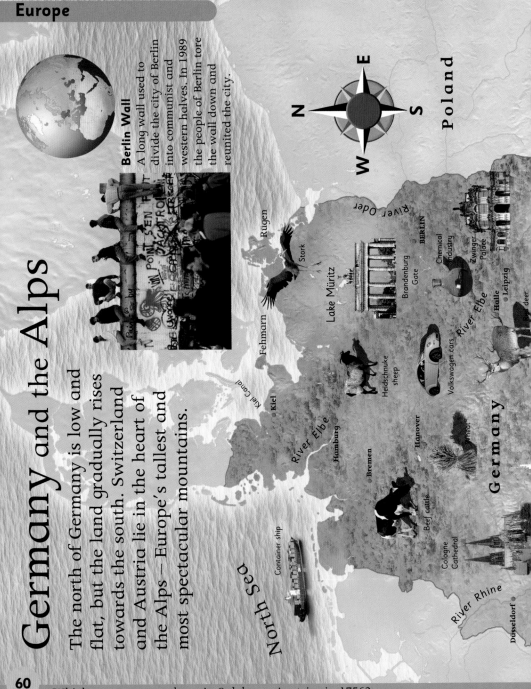

Germany and the Alps

The north of Germany is low and flat, but the land gradually rises towards the south. Switzerland and Austria lie in the heart of the Alps – Europe's tallest and most spectacular mountains.

Berlin Wall
A long wall used to divide the city of Berlin into communist and western halves. In 1989 the people of Berlin tore the wall down and reunited the city.

Poland

N E S W

River Oder

Rügen

Stork

BERLIN

Chemical industry

Zwinger Palace

Leipzig

Brandenburg Gate

Halle

Red deer

Lake Müritz

River Elbe

Volkswagen cars

Fehmarn

Heidschnuke sheep

Kiel Canal

Kiel

Germany

River Elbe

Hanover

Wheat

Hamburg

Bremen

Beef cattle

Container ship

North Sea

Cologne Cathedral

River Rhine

Düsseldorf

Which composer was born in Salzburg, Austria, in 1756?

Czech
Republic

Neusiedler Lake

VIENNA

Mountain
climbing

Graz

Linz

Danube

River Danube

Austria

Austrian Alps

Snow
boarding

Salzburg

Lake
Chiemsee

Chamois
goat

Thuringian
Forest

Bohemian Forest

Nuremberg

Oktoberfest

Munich

Bavarian Alps

Innsbruck

Marmot

River Main

River Rhine

Frankfurt

Mannheim

Heidelberg

Wine

Mercedes

Stuttgart

Swabian Alps

River Danube

Ulm

Cheese

Neuschwanstein
Castle

Zugspitze
2,962 m
(9,718 ft)

Liechtenstein

VADUZ

Davos

Frankfurt
skyline

Black Forest

Freiburg

Lake Constance

Zurich

Swiss
army knife

Swiss Alps

Alpine
horn

France

Chocolate

BERN

Geneva

River Rhône

Matterhorn
4,478 m
(14,692 ft)

Switzerland

Germany and the Alps

Germany, Austria, and Switzerland are rich industrial countries. They make and export many high-quality goods, including cars, watches, and chocolates.

Pyramid peak

The Matterhorn in Switzerland is one of the tallest mountains in the Alps. Some people have fallen to their death trying to climb it.

Ice has carved the peak of the Matterhorn into a pyramid shape.

German industry

Volkswagens are made in Europe's biggest car factory, near Hanover in Germany. Car-making is one of Germany's main industries.

Winter sports

Millions of people come to the Alps every winter to ski and snowboard. Hikers and mountaineers walk in the valleys and scale the peaks.

How did farmers used to communicate in the Alps?

Alpine wildlife

Many plants and animals survive high in the Alps.

Edelweiss is a small flower that grows in Alpine meadows.

The **Alpine marmot** sleeps through the winter in its burrow.

The **chamois** grows a thick, woolly coat to keep it warm.

Neuschwanstein in Bavaria was the inspiration for Sleeping Beauty's castle in Disneyland.

German castles

Fabulous castles are scattered among the mountains of southern Germany. Neuschwanstein was built in 1869 by an eccentric king called Ludwig II.

Carnival time

Germans celebrate the end of winter with carnivals. In Cologne, people dress up in bright costumes and join the parades.

Viennese pastries are said to be the best cakes in the world.

Viennese coffee houses

Vienna in Austria is famous for its coffee houses, where people drink coffee and eat expensive cakes.

Alpine cows have bells so that farmers don't lose them on the mountainside.

Germany's waterways

Germany's cities are linked by a large network of canals and rivers. This cargo barge is on the River Neckar in the city of Heidelberg.

Swiss people eat more chocolate than anyone else in the world.

Dairy farming

Swiss farmers take their cows to high alpine meadows in summer. The cows' milk is used for making chocolates and cheese.

By yodelling (singing across mountain valleys).

Spain and Portugal

Spain and Portugal are in the sunny southwest corner of Europe. Together they make up a region called the Iberian Peninsula.

Azores

These Portuguese islands are in the Atlantic, about a third of the way to the USA.

Dolphin

Ponta Delgada

Madeira

The Portuguese island of Madeira is famous for making a rich type of wine also called Madeira.

Grapes

Funchal

Canary Islands

These seven Spanish islands are off the west coast of Africa.

La Palma

Santa Cruz de Tenerife

Tenerife

Fuerteventura

Lanzarote

Gran Canaria

Banana plantations

Mountain bike

Rain

Santiago

Santiago Cathedral

León

Coal mine

Atlantic Ocean

Oporto

Clay cockerel (symbol of Portugal)

Salamanca

Coimbra

Windmills

Portugal

River

Belem Tower

LISBON

Sheep

Badajoz

Packing fish

Flamenco dancer

Tourists

Algarve

Lagos

Faro

Seville

Crayfish

Wind surfing

Lynx

Baetic

Gibraltar

Which is the rainiest city in Spain?

France

Andorra

ANDORRA
LA VELLA

Guggenheim
Museum

Bilbao

Basque
Country

Mountain
goat

Pyrenees

Skiing

Wild boar

Barcelona

alladolid

Spain

Iberian Mountains

River Ebro

Rioja wine

Sagrada Familia
Cathedral, Barcelona

N

W   E

S

Roman aqueduct

Sardines

Balearic Islands

Minorca

Mahón

MADRID

Majorca

Palma

Tagus

Bull-fighting

Paella

Mediterranean Sea

Royal Palace

Valencia

Ibiza

Albacete

Ibiza

Oranges

Formentera

Alicante

Guadalquivir

Costa Blanca

Andalusian horse

Cartagena

Andalusia

Guitar

Majorca
The Spanish
island of Majorca
is one of Europe's top
tourist destinations.
Its rugged coast has lots
of picturesque beaches.

Mountains

Granada

Olives
and oil

Malaga

Costa del Sol

Jet ski

Santiago.

Spain and Portugal

The streets of Spain and Portugal burst to life during their colourful festivals, or fiestas, but in the hot afternoons they can be sleepy and quiet.

Flamenco dresses have colourful frills.

Unfinished cathedral
This unusual building is an unfinished cathedral in the Spanish city of Barcelona. It was designed by a famous Spanish architect, Antonio Gaudí (1852–1926).

Bulls in the streets
Running from charging bulls is part of a festival held every July in the city of Pamplona. Hundreds of men run away from bulls that are let out in the streets.

Spanish dancing
The flamenco is a traditional dance with lots of twirling and stamping. It started in southern Spain about 500 years ago.

Paella
This traditional Spanish dish is made from yellow rice mixed with seafood, pieces of meat, tomatoes, and peppers.

Which city held the 1992 Olympic Games?

The guitar is played by plucking the strings.

Algarve beaches

Portugal's southern coast is called the Algarve. This warm area has many sandy beaches and it is a popular spot with holiday-makers from the rest of Europe.

Classical guitar

Traditional Spanish music, including flamenco, is played on the classical guitar. The guitar was invented in Spain about 500 years ago.

Fishing industry

Bordered by the Atlantic Ocean and the Mediterranean Sea, Spain and Portugal have huge fishing industries. People who live on the coast eat lots of fish and seafood.

Traditional Portuguese fishing boats.

A2307M

A2220.M

Lobsters turn red when they are cooked. Living lobsters are blue-grey.

Barcelona.

Italy

Italy is shaped like a boot, with the top in the Alps mountains and the toe swimming in the Mediterranean Sea. The Apennine mountains run like a bone down the leg.

Italian lakes

There are 23 lakes in the lake district in northern Italy. Lake Garda is the biggest, and a popular place to sail and windsurf.

Skier

Dolomites

Venice

Venetian gondola

Tagliatelli carbonara

San Marino

A l p s

Mountain goat

Lake Garda

River Po

Ferrari

Bologna

Florence

Florence Cathedral

Pisa

Moped

Milan

Wine

Leaning Tower of Pisa

Turin

Fishing boat

Tuna

How many islands make up Malta?

Octopus

Crab

Wine

Taranto

Olives and olive oil

Sheep

Oranges

Almonds

Pescara

Apennines

Italy

Mount Vesuvius

Pompeii

Cast of a body at Pompeii

Squid

Messina

Noto Cathedral

Pizza

Naples

Amalfi

Scuba diving

Syracuse

Vatican City

The Colosseum (Rome)

ROME

Can you find...

Europe's largest volcano?
Mount Etna in Sicily is also Europe's most active volcano.

The world's most wonky tower?
The Leaning Tower of Pisa is a campanile, or bell tower.

Where the first pizza was made? A baker in Naples invented the pizza in the 1800s.

Mount Etna

Palermo

Sicily

Agrigento

Temple of Castor and Pollux

VALLETTA

Malta

Lemons

Mediterranean Sea

Sardines

Sardinia

Tourism

Wild boar

Cagliari

Amalfi

Italy

Italy has some of the world's most beautiful cities, and its museums contain priceless paintings and sculptures. Italy also has modern industries, such as car-making and electronics.

Vatican City

The Vatican City is the home of the Pope, the head of the Roman Catholic Church. It is the world's smallest state and has its own flag.

The Grand Canal is the main "street" in Venice. It is lined with palaces build by rich merchants.

A Venetian boat is called a gondola.

Venice

The ancient city of Venice is built on islands in the sea. Venice has canals and boats instead of streets and cars.

What were the people who lived in ancient Italy called?

Italian food

Italians enjoy eating with family and friends. Most meals include fresh vegetables and olive oil.

Cappuccino is coffee with frothy milk. Italians drink many different kinds of coffee.

Pasta is made in dozens of different shapes. This shape is called farfalle.

Ice cream has been made in Italy for more than 500 years.

Painted chapel

The Sistine Chapel is in the Vatican. It was painted about 500 years ago by great Italian painters, including the famous artist and sculptor Michelangelo.

get going

Make a pizza from a piece of bread with some sliced tomatoes and cheese on top. Cook it under the grill or in the oven until the cheese melts.

Mount Vesuvius

The cast of a dog killed at Pompeii

Vesuvius and Pompeii

In the year AD 79, a volcano called Mount Vesuvius erupted and buried the town of Pompeii in ash. The ruins of Pompeii and the remains of the volcano's victims can still be seen today.

It took Michelangelo four years to paint the ceiling of the Sistine Chapel, between 1508 and 1512.

Cars and scooters

Many famous makes of sports car come from Italy. This is a Ferrari. The streets of Italian towns and cities are full of buzzing scooters.

Central Eastern Europe

These countries were under communist rule until the 1990s. Today they are modern nations with thriving industries. Traditional farming continues in the rural areas.

Did you know?

The Polish town of Torun is well-known for its **gingerbread**.

Budapest is split by the Danube. Buda is on one bank, Pest on the other.

The snow-white **Lipizzaner horse** is bred in Slovenia.

Baltic Sea

Ship building

Koszalin

Gdansk

Windmills

Szczecin

Canoeing

Mazury lakes

European bison

Chemical industry

Market Square Warsaw

Lublin

Sugar beet

River Vistula

WARSAW

Skiing

Kielce

Krakow

Torun

Gingerbread

Lodz

Poland

Potato farming

Poznań

Mining

Pig farms

River Oder

Wroclaw

Cattle farms

Charles Bridge

Karlovy Vary

PRAGUE

Pizen

Hradec Kralove

River Elbe

Germany

What ingredient makes Hungarian goulash spicy?

High Tatra Mountains
This mountain range lies in Poland and Slovakia, and forms part of the Carpathian Mountains. The tallest peak is 2,655 m (8,710 ft) high.

Paprika.

Central Eastern Europe

Winters bring deep snow to the plains and mountains of this part of Europe. Summers bring tourists to visit some of Europe's best preserved cities.

European bison

Vltava River, Prague

Old and modern

The capital of the Czech Republic is the historic city of Prague. It is full of ancient buildings because it has never been damaged by war.

Lake Bled bell

This is Lake Bled in Slovenia. Legend says that ringing the bell in the tower makes your wish come true.

Bison

About 1,000 wild bison live in Poland's forests. One of these enormous animals weighs as much as a family car.

Puppet performers

The Czechs love the theatre. Puppet theatre is especially popular here and in Slovakia.

What is the Czech word for "yes"?

Painted presents

Czechs and Slovaks give each other coloured eggs at Easter. They are hard-boiled and painted by hand.

Dubrovnik's walled defences.

Hot spring baths

Budapest is famous for its thermal baths. They are filled with hot water from underground springs. Bathing in the water is supposed to heal diseases.

Puppets

Dubrovnik

This ancient walled city is on the Croatian coast. Millions of people come here to walk in the narrow streets and enjoy the cool sea air.

Eastern Europe

The countries of eastern Europe lie between the Baltic Sea and the Black Sea. They were part of the Soviet Union, but became independent states in 1991.

Hill of Crosses

This sacred site in Lithuania is visited by lots of pilgrims every year. They leave crosses on the hill to show their devotion to Christianity.

Russian Federation

Vitsyebsk

Polatsk

Pskov

Estonia

TALLINN

Lake Peipus

Golden eagle

Latvia

RIGA

Bauska

Latvian costume

Liepāja

Amber jewellery

Cruise ship

Baltic Sea

Hill of Crosses

The centre of Europe

Trakai Castle

Lithuania

VILNIUS

Sugar beet

Flax

Belarus

MINSK

Poland

What are the Baltic States?

Coal mining
• Donets'k

Sea of Azov

• Kerch

Crimea

• Yalta

Swallow's
Nest
Castle

Black sea
tourism

Black Sea

Sunflowers

Dnipropetrovs'k •

White geese

Kharkiv •

River Dnieper

Wheat

St Andrew's Church

Chernihiv •

Homyel •

KIEV •

Mushroom
picking

Wooden church

Gymnastic
school

Odesa •

Chornobyl •

Mammoth fossils

Pripet Marshes

Mink

Ukraine

Potatoes

CHISINAU •

Wooden Moldovian
gateway

Moldova

L'viv •

Ukranian folk dancers

Chernivtsi •

Carpathian
Mountains

Romania

Can you find...

Ukraine's oldest creatures?
Mammoths walked the Earth
25,000 years ago.

The plant used to make linen?
Flax is a major crop of Belarus. Its
fibres are made into linen clothes.

Europe's largest marshland?
The Pripet Marshes cover 270,000
square kilometres (104,000 sq miles).

Estonia, Latvia, and Lithuania – the countries bordering the Baltic Sea.

77

Eastern Europe

The cold Baltic Sea makes Estonia, Latvia, and Lithuania damp and chilly. Ukraine is rich in natural resources such as oil, gas, coal, and metal ores.

The ancient city of Tallinn is Estonia's main port.

Rural life

Modern industries are growing in eastern Europe, but many people still live off the land. Farmers work with hand tools and horses rather than machines and tractors.

Estonian capital

Only a million people live in the hilly, wet country of Estonia. A third of them live in the capital, Tallinn.

Luge tracks are covered in ice.

Rhythmic gymnasts twirl ribbons and hoops as they leap about.

Latvian luge

Near Riga in Latvia is a huge bobsleigh and luge track used for international races. Competitors hurtle down it at up to 125 kph (78 mph).

Dancing gymnasts

Rhythmic gymnastics is a very popular sport in Ukraine. It is a combination of gymnastics and dance, set to music.

What is the world's most expensive caviar called?

Lithuanian amber

Amber is a kind of gem that forms over millions of years from conifer tree resin. Sometimes it has tiny creatures trapped inside it. Nearly all of the world's amber comes from mines in northern Lithuania.

This spider became trapped in amber millions of years ago.

Castle on the coast

One of the best known sights in southern Ukraine is Swallow's Nest Castle on the coast of Crimea. It used to be the home of a German oil tycoon but is now an Italian restaurant.

Swallow's Nest Castle is perched on a cliff overlooking the Black Sea.

Wolves

Grey wolves have been killed off in most of Europe, but packs of wolves still roam free in the Carpathian Mountains in southwestern Ukraine. They hunt wild boar and deer in mountain forests.

Traditional food

These are some of the traditional dishes eaten in Eastern Europe.

Draniki is made from potato pancakes stuffed with meat.

Caviar is an expensive delicacy made from the eggs of sturgeon fish.

Borsht is beetroot soup. It is eaten hot or cold.

Black Sea tourism

Many Eastern Europeans and Russians spend their summer holidays in Crimea, which has warm weather, miles of beaches, and dramatic, hilly scenery.

Almas caviar. It is shimmering white and costs £14,000 per kilogram.

Southeast Europe

The mighty River Danube winds its way across southeast Europe, forming a natural border between Romania and Bulgaria. Further south are the scattered ruins of the cities of Ancient Greece.

Black Sea

River Danube

Varna

Bran Castle
Transylvania

Wolf

Natural yoghurt

Burgas

Carpathian Mountains

BUCHAREST

Ruse

Folk dancers
at Kazanluk
Festival of Roses

Alexander
Nevsky
Cathedral

Kazanluk

Roses

Sibiu

Romania

Pleven

SOFIA

Bulgaria

Satu Mare

Wild boar

Transylvanian Alps

Parliament Palace

Goats

Timişoara

BELGRADE

Traditional
Serbian costume

Pristina

SKOPJE

Macedonia

Serbian
Ražnjiči Kebab

Serbia and
Montenegro

Grapes

Bosnia and
Herzegovina

SARAJEVO

Dinaric Alps

Oranges

Banja Luka

Statue in
Liberation
Square, Sarajevo

Mostar

Adriatic Sea

What is Greece's most important crop?

N E S W

Turkey

Rhodes

Sponge

Bouzouki

Dolphins

Lesbos

Chíos

Aegean Sea

Cyclades Islands

Knossos Palace

• Iráklion

Crete

Greece

Salonika •

Olive oil

ATHENS •

Parthenon

Ceremonial soldier from Athens

Mediterranean Sea

Bitola •

Greek coffee

Greek vase

Patras •

Peloponnese

Greek church

Pindus Mountains

Albania

Cephalonia

Zakinthos

Watermelon

Sailing ship

Octopus

Can you find...

A sponge? Old-fashioned bathroom sponges are the skeletons of dead sea creatures.

Yoghurt? People in Bulgaria eat lots of yoghurt because they think it helps them live longer.

Greek coffee? Greek people make coffee by boiling ground coffee in a tiny pan of water until it foams.

Chios Island in the Aegean Sea

Olives.

Southeast Europe

Southeast Europe is hot and hilly, with miles of sunny beaches. Many of the people are farmers, but the tourism is also important. People from all over the world visit Greece to see its ancient ruins and visit its islands.

Greek soldiers
This soldier is called an Evzone. He is a guard at the Greek parliament building in Athens.

Food

Many crops are grown in this part of Europe.

Grapes for making wine grow well in the warm climate.

Watermelons are refreshing fruits that grow on the ground.

Maize is grown for flour, animal food, and as a fuel.

The Parthenon
This ancient temple stands on a rocky outcrop in the centre of Athens. It was built nearly 2,500 years ago.

White-washed churches dot the sunny islands of Greece.

Greek islands
Greece has more than 2,000 sun-baked islands. Millions of Europeans come here on holiday.

What major sporting tournament began in Greece in 776 BC?

Bran Castle,
Transylvania

Rose festival
Bulgarian farmers grow roses for making perfume. About 2,000 petals are needed to make just one gram of rose-oil. The rose-pickers hold a festival every year at harvest time.

Rose-picking festival in June at Kazanluk, Bulgaria

The legend of Dracula
Transylvania is a region in the north of Romania. The mountains here are covered with forests. Transylvania was the home of a vampire in the novel *Dracula*.

Goat farming
Farming is hard work in the dry heat of Greece. Many farmers keep a herd of goats for cheese and milk.

Dancing gypsy
Southeast Europe has many Romany people (gypsies). They spend their lives travelling, and they love traditional music and dance.

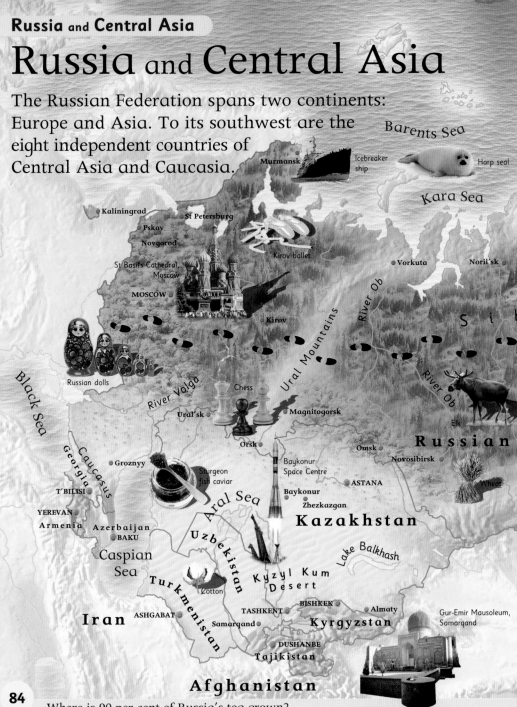

Russia and Central Asia

The Russian Federation spans two continents:
Europe and Asia. To its southwest are the
eight independent countries of
Central Asia and Caucasia.

Barents Sea

Murmansk

Icebreaker
ship

Harp seal

Kara Sea

Kaliningrad

St Petersburg

Pskov

Novgorod

Vorkuta

Noril'sk

St Basil's Cathedral,
Moscow

MOSCOW

Kirov ballet

River Ob

S i b

Kirov

Ural Mountains

River Ob

Russian dolls

River Volga

Chess

Ural'sk

Magnitogorsk

Elk

R u s s i a n

Black Sea

Orsk

Omsk

Novosibirsk

Caucasus

Georgia

Groznyy

Sturgeon
fish caviar

Baykonur
Space Centre

ASTANA

Wheat

T'BILISI

Baykonur

YEREVAN

Aral Sea

Zhezkazgan

Armenia

Azerbaijan

Kazakhstan

BAKU

Uzbekistan

Caspian
Sea

Lake Balkhash

Turkmenistan

Kyzyl Kum
Desert

Cotton

Iran

ASHGABAT

Samarqand

TASHKENT

BISHKEK

Almaty

Kyrgyzstan

Gur-Emir Mausoleum,
Samarqand

DUSHANBE

Tajikistan

Afghanistan

Where is 90 per cent of Russia's tea grown?

Russia and Central Asia

Arctic Ocean

Pevek

Brent geese

Walrus

Nenet people

River Lena

Yakut people

Reindeer

Walkabout

Russia is the world's widest country. It would take more than two months to cross if you walked non-stop from west to east.

Verkhoyansk

Wolf

Magadan

Kamchatka Peninsula

Salmon

Yakutsk

Okhotsk

Brown bear

e r i a

Sea of Okhotsk

N

W E

S

Diamonds

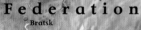
Timber

Mining

F e d e r a t i o n

Bratsk

Trans-Siberian railway

Khabarovsk

Irkutsk

Lake Baikal

Freshwater seal

China

Siberian tiger

Vladivostok

Did you know?

Caviar from the Caspian Sea is so expensive it is known as "black gold".

Lake Baikal is the world's deepest, and largest, freshwater lake.

Verkhoyansk is the world's coldest town. In winter the temperature falls to -68˚C (-90˚F).

A shrinking sea

The Aral Sea, between Kazakhstan and Uzbekistan, is shrinking. The water is being used on Uzbekistan's cotton fields, stranding fishing boats.

Georgia.

85

Russia

Russia is the world's largest country. Most people live in cities in the west, near the rest of Europe. Russia is governed from Moscow.

The Summer Palace

This magnificent palace is in St Petersburg. It was built 300 years ago for Peter the Great, who was the ruler, or tsar, of Russia.

Russian churches have domed roofs shaped like onions.

St Basil's

St Basil's Cathedral is in Red Square, Moscow. Churches are important to Russians. Three-quarters of Russians follow the Russian Orthodox branch of Christianity.

Russian dolls fit inside each other.

What was St Petersburg called when Russia was in the Soviet Union?

Ballet school

The Bolshoi Ballet is Russia's most famous ballet company. Dancers trained at its ballet school perform at the Bolshoi Theatre in Moscow.

Russian culture

Culture is very important in Russia, especially music, art, theatre, and literature.

Tchaikovsky and **Stravinsky**, both famous composers, were born in Russia.

The Russian writer **Tolstoy** wrote the famous novel *War and Peace*.

The **balalaika** is a traditional Russian instrument. It is played by plucking its strings.

Soviet Russia

Russia once belonged to a huge federation called the Soviet Union. The Kremlin in Moscow was its seat of government.

The Kremlin is an enormous fortress in Moscow.

The red star, hammer, and sickle were the symbols of the Soviet Union.

Brown bear

The brown bear is the symbol of Russia. It lives in the north, hunting fish and small animals.

Vladimir Ilyich Lenin (1870–1924) was the leader who founded the Soviet Union.

Siberia and neighbours

Siberia is a vast area of pine forests to the east of the Ural mountains. Northern Siberia is so cold that the ground is frozen all year round.

Tents of Siberian reindeer herders

Reindeer
This ivory carving from Siberia shows a reindeer pulling a sledge. People in northern Siberia keep reindeer for milk, meat, and fur, as well as for pulling sledges.

Nenets children wear fur coats and fur-lined boots.

Siberian people
The Nenets live in the forests of Siberia in winter. In summer they pack up their tents and travel north with reindeer herds to pasture in the Arctic.

The Trans-Siberian railway
It takes eight days to travel from Moscow to Vladivostok along the Trans-Siberian railway. It's the longest railway line in the world.

How long is the Trans-Siberian railway?

Made in Russia

Here are some of the well-known objects made by Russia's craftspeople.

A **samovar** is a decorated urn for heating water for tea.

Antique jewellery **Fabergé eggs** are worth a fortune.

Clay dolls have been made for the Dymkovo village fair for many years.

Warm **boots** are made from the furs of Siberian forest animals.

Many Russian **toys** were traditionally carved from wood.

Russian Rockets

Baykonur Space Centre in Kazakhstan is the home of Russia's space programme, and where they launch their rockets. Sputnik, the first man-made space satellite, was launched here in 1957.

Rockets lift off from Baykonur Space Centre.

The top of the rocket carries a satellite or supplies for astronauts already in space.

Engines push the rocket upwards.

Oil in Azerbaijan

There is a lot of oil, gas, coal, and other materials under the ground in Azerbaijan in Central Asia. Azerbaijan gets most of its money by selling oil.

Weaving carpets

Central Asian women weave decorative woollen carpets to give as wedding presents. The carpets are made by hand and coloured with plant dyes.

Middle East

This part of the world is hot and dry, with large deserts. Three of the world's great religions began here.

Istanbul

Blue Mosque   ANKAR

Turkey

Mediterranean Sea

NICOSI
Cyprus

Sculpted
menorah
Jerusalem

Mecca

The holiest place for a Muslim is the Ka'ba, a cube-shaped shrine in Mecca. Muslims face the Ka'ba when they pray and try to visit it at least once in their lifetime.

World's first skyscrapers

The people of Yemen started building mud-brick skyscrapers thousands of years ago. The ground floors are used for animals or for storing goods. Families live in the upper floors.

Fruits of the desert

Farmers can grow crops only in the wettest parts of the Middle East.

Figs are soft, sticky fruits that can be dried to make them last longer.

Olives are grown for their seeds, which are pressed to make olive oil.

Dates are the fruit of palm trees, which grow by rivers and in oases.

Which country produces 65 per cent of the world's hazelnuts?

Black Sea

Whirling
dervish dancer

Head of Zeus

Mount Ararat
5,165 m ▲
(16,945 ft)

Caspian Sea

Syria

Olives

Figs

DAMASCUS

EIRUT

AMMAN

RUSALEM

Israel

Lebanon

Jordan

Iraq

BAGHDAD

Marsh Arab reed house

Chador, traditional
dress for women

TEHRAN

Iran

Turquoise

Iranian food – chicken kebab

Falconry

Ancient city
of Petra

Kuwait
KUWAIT
CITY

The Gulf

Persepolis palace

Desert
oasis

Mecca

RIYADH

Oil

Bahrain

Qatar

DOHA

ABU DHABI

Oman

Gulf of Oman

MUSCAT

United
Arab Emirates

Oil refinery

Red Sea

Saudi Arabia

Arabian desert

Oman

Coral reefs grow
along the coast
of the Red Sea,
where the water
is warm and clear.

Mecca

Camels

Desert oryx

Oil tanker

N

W   E

S

Yemen

SANA

Frankincense tree

Arabian Sea

Middle East

The Middle East lies at the crossroads between Europe, Africa, and Asia. Most of the people are Muslims – followers of the religion of Islam.

Middle Eastern treat

Baklava is a popular Middle Eastern pastry. It is made from rolled layers of thin pastry and chopped nuts, covered with sticky honey.

The towers around a mosque are called minarets. This is the Blue Mosque in Istanbul, Turkey.

Mosques

Muslims pray in buildings called mosques. Mosques are decorated with patterned tiles and verses from the Muslim holy book, the Qur'an.

Patterned Islamic tile

Traditional dress

Muslim women hide their hair and the shape of their body with loose-fitting clothes when they go out in public.

Camels can last for ten months

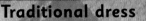

Camel train carrying cargo across the desert

What language is spoken in most of the Middle East?

Oil wealth

More than half the world's oil lies under the ground in the Middle East. The discovery of oil and gas has made many of the countries in the Middle East very rich. They sell lots of oil to other countries, some of which is turned into petrol for cars.

The Western Wall

Jerusalem is a holy city for Muslims, Christians, and Jews. Jews pray at the Western Wall. It is the only part that is left of a Jewish temple that was built 2,000 years ago.

Salty sea

The Dead Sea is 400 metres (1,300 ft) below sea level. It is so salty that people can float in the water. Plants and animals cannot survive in it.

Burj Al-Arab hotel in Dubai, United Arab Emirates

World's tallest hotel

The Burj-Al-Arab hotel in Dubai is the world's tallest hotel. It was built on an artificial island and designed to look like the sail of a ship.

Arab men wear long, baggy clothes and a headdress to shade them from the hot desert sun.

get going

Make an Arab headdress. Fold a chequered tablecloth diagonally in half and hang it over your head, leaving your face clear. Then tie it in place with dark belt or ribbon.

without a drink of water.

Southern Asia

Southern Asia is colourful and crowded. India is the biggest country in the region, with a population of more than a billion.

Elephants on parade

During the festival of Puram in southern India, 101 elephants march through the town of Trichur in a grand parade.

Snow leopard

Lapis lazuli

Afghanistan

Herat

KABUL

Decorated lorry

Tomb of Muhammad Ali Jinnah

Pakistan

Quetta

Multan

ISLAMABAD

Golden Temple

Dancer

Hyderabad

Karachi

Green turtles

Taj Mahal

Camel market

Surat

India

River Narmada

Rickshaw

Delhi
NEW DELHI

Agra

River Ganges

River dolphin

Sacred cow

Nepal

Tea picking

Imphal

DHAKA

Bangladesh

Chittagong

Calcutta

94

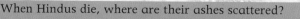
When Hindus die, where are their ashes scattered?

Coconut tree and coconut

Andaman Islands (India)

Nicobar Islands (India)

Bay of Bengal

Fishing boat

Cuttack

Raipur

Common lobster

Herring

The Monsoon

Southern Asia is normally hot and dry, but every summer it pours down for weeks. This rainy season, called the monsoon, helps farmers grow crops like rice.

Tiger

Vijayawada

Thresher shark

Nagpur

Chennai (Madras)

Sri Lanka

Jaffna

Kandy

Tea leaves

Snake charmer

Kathkali Dancer

COLOMBO

Trichur

Indian elephant

Calicut

Mumbai (Bombay)

Arabian Sea

Tuna fish

Can you find...

Lapis lazuli? This precious stone was once used to make brilliant, sky-blue paint.

An Indian dancer? Classical dancers use movements of their bodies to tell ancient stories.

Ganges river dolphin? This dolphin is almost blind and finds its way in muddy water by sound.

In the River Ganges.

95

Southern Asia

Different cultures and religions mix together in Southern Asia. Most people are Hindus, but there are also Muslims, Buddhists, Sikhs, and Christians.

Indian food
Traditional Indian meals consist of lots of separate dishes on a metal plate called a thali.

Spicy chicken
Dumplings
Vegetables
Lentil soup
Bread
Rice
Raita (yoghurt dip)
Poppadoms

Pilgrims bathing in the Ganges

Disappearing tigers
Tigers once lived all over southern Asia, but today they are rare because of hunting. Parts of India and Bangladesh still have man-eating tigers.

Four minarets surround the central tomb.

Indian arts
Indian people enjoy music, dance, theatre, and story telling. In the art of Kathakali, dancers act out Hindu myths.

Kathakali dancer

The Holy Ganges
The River Ganges is sacred to Hindus. They believe that the river's water washes away their sins. Millions of pilgrims bathe at the holy city of Varanasi.

What is the main crop in Sri Lanka?

Bollywood

So many films are made in Bombay (Mumbai) that people call this town Bollywood. Indian films are very long and feature lots of singing and dancing.

The Elephant God Ganesh

Taj Mahal

The Taj Mahal is a tomb. An Indian emperor called Shah Jahan built it more than 300 years ago for his favourite wife when she died.

Hindu gods

Hindus worship many gods. Statues of Ganesh, the elephant god, are placed near entrances to houses.

get going

Make some raita (Indian yoghurt dip). Put some plain yoghurt in a small dish. Grate some cucumber and mix it into the yoghurt. Add a sprinkling of coriander leaves or mint.

Tea.

Southeast Asia

Southeast Asia is hot and rainy all year round. There are thousands of islands, and many are covered with steamy rainforests and towering volcanoes.

China

Elephant

Burma (Myanmar)

Thai dancer

Rubies

HANOI

Laos

VIENTIANE

RANGOON

Vietnam

Thailand

Sampan boat

BANGKOK

Angkor Wat

South China Sea

Tapir

Cambodia

Pearls

PHNOM PENH

Ho Chi Minh

Floating market
The city of Bangkok is riddled with canals. Traders sell their goods from boats and shoppers paddle by to look for bargains.

Orchid

Omar Ali Saifuddin Mosque

Petronas Towers

Brunei

BANDAR SERI BEGAW

Tiger

KUALA LUMPUR

Malaysia

Singapore

Sumatra

Orang-utan

Borneo

Cocon

Padang

Indo

Rafflesia (giant flower)

JAKARTA

Java

Shadow puppets

What is the largest lizard in the world?

Can you find...

A very rare kind of ape? **Orang-utans** live only in Borneo and Sumatra.

An animal with tusks that grow through its face? The **babirusa** is a kind of pig.

The world's largest flower? **Rafflesia** grows to nearly a metre (3 feet) wide.

N
W E
S

Planting rice

MANILA

Vinta boats

Philippines

Cebu

Water buffalo

Pacific Ocean

Davao

Tuna

Celebes Sea

Babirusa

Celebes

Moluccas

Nutmeg

Ambon

Toraja house

n **e** **s** **i** **a**

DILI

East Timor

Komodo dragon

Rice paddies

The wet climate is ideal for growing rice. Farmers plant it in flooded fields called paddies, which are sometimes built like steps in the sides of hills.

Jayapura

New Guinea

Conch shell

Papua New Guinea

Asmat warrior

PORT MORESBY

Mangoes

The Komodo dragon. It can grow to 3 m (10 ft) long.

Southeast Asia

The 10 countries of Southeast Asia are spread over islands and mainland. The smallest is the island state of Singapore. The biggest is Indonesia, which has more than 13,000 islands.

Reclining Buddha

Many Southeast Asians are Buddhists. Their religion was founded by a man called the Buddha 2,500 years ago. Statues of reclining Buddhas show him on his death-bed.

Reclining Buddha in Ayuthaya, Thailand   Buddhist monk

Temple in the jungle

The magnificent temple of Angkor Wat in Cambodia was built 900 years ago. It was hidden by overgrown jungle until archaeologists cleared the trees last century.

Angkor Wat's towers are shown on Cambodia's national flag.

New Guinea

Hundreds of tribes live among the jungle-covered mountains of New Guinea, and many have a unique language. This girl is from the Mount Hagen tribe.

What smelly fruit is banned from many restaurants in Southeast Asia?

Exotic Fruit

Tropical fruits grow well in Southeast Asia's warm, wet climate.

The **durian** tastes delicious but smells disgusting.

Inside a **coconut** is white flesh and a hole filled with liquid.

The **custard apple** has cream-coloured flesh like thick custard.

Slices of **starfruit** make star-shaped decorations for puddings.

The **rambutan** has a tough skin covered with soft hairs.

The Petronas Towers

These office blocks in Kuala Lumpur, Malaysia, were the world's tallest buildings from 1998 until 2003. Each tower is 452 m (1,483 ft) tall.

Island wildlife

Many extraordinary animals and plants live in Southeast Asia. Orang-utans live in rainforests on Borneo and Sumatra. Komodo dragons are flesh-eating lizards found on a few islands in Indonesia.

Long-necked women

The Karen tribe live in the hills of Burma. The women stretch their necks as they grow up by wearing neck rings.

Orang-utans swing on flimsy trees and branches to move through the forest.

Komodo dragon

China and neighbours

Over 1 billion people live in China – that's one-fifth of the world's people. Next door, Mongolia has the fewest people for its size.

Terracotta Army

This army of statues in Xi'an was made more than 2,000 years ago to guard the tomb of Qin Shi Huang, China's first emperor. The statues were rediscovered in 1974.

Chinese opera

Chinese opera has lots of singing, acting, and acrobatics. Make-up is used to show the type of character being played.

N
W E
S

Altay

Mongolian ger (house)

Yining

Urumqi

Bactrian camel

Turpan   Hami

Kashi

Ibex

K2

Yak

Tibet

Patala Palace

Bhairabnath Temple

Himalayas

Lhasa

KATHMANDU   Mount Everest

Nepal

THIMPU
Bhutan

Can you find...

The world's tallest mountain? Mount Everest is 8,850 metres (29,035 ft) tall.

The world's most crowded place? Hong Kong has 6,000 people per square kilometre (2,300 per square mile).

China's hottest place? Turpan has recorded temperatures of up to 47°C (117°F).

What is the world's second-tallest mountain?

Russian Federation

Mongolia

ULAN BATOR

Dinosaur fossils

Gobi Desert

Harbin

Snow sculptures at the
Harbin Ice Festival

Jinlin

Shenyang

North Korea

PYONGYANG

Temple of Heaven

Dalian

SEOUL

South
Korea

BEIJING

Seoul Olympic
Stadium

Qingdao

Korea
Strait

Great Wall of China

China

Yellow River

East China
Sea

Lanzhou

Xi'an

Shanghai

Tibetan
monk

Tea plantation

Hanzhou

Wuhan

River Yangtze

Chengdu

China porcelain

Changsha

Silk moth

Fuzhou

Junk (fishing boat)

TAIPEI

Taiwan

Hong Kong business district
and Exhibition Centre

Electronic
goods

Red panda

Kunming

Giant panda

Hong Kong

Nanning

South China Sea

Hainan

K2 in the Himalayas. It is 8,611 metres (28,250 ft) tall.

103

Eastern China and Korea

China is a vast and ancient country. Emperors ruled it for thousands of years, but today it has a communist government. Korea is split into two countries: North Korea and South Korea.

Packed Hong Kong
Hong Kong is a small and crowded region of China. It is an important centre for banking and commerce.

Staple food
Rice is the main crop, and the most important source of food, in China and Korea. Eastern China's rainy climate is ideal for rice, which grows best in flooded fields.

Rice is eaten with chopsticks.

Great Wall
More than 500 years ago, the Chinese built the Great Wall of China to keep out invaders from Mongolia. It is the longest man-made structure in the world.

Rice farm

On your bike
There are millions of bicycles in China, especially in rural areas. In cities such as Beijing there are more cars. Bicycles are also used as taxis and market stalls.

What are Chinese years named after?

Martial arts

Chinese and Korean people have turned fighting into an art form. One of the most popular martial arts in Korea is tae kwon do, which is used for self-defence or sport. Kicking and punching are allowed.

The misty Guilin mountains are said to be the most beautiful place in China.

Chinese New Year   Tae kwon do fighters

The most important festival in China is the Chinese New Year, when people celebrate the return of spring. One of the main events is a parade led by a huge dancing dragon.

The Chinese dragon is a symbol of strength and good luck.

Guilin Mountains

The town of Guilin in southern China is surrounded by small, pointy mountains that are often shrouded in mist. They are a favourite subject for Chinese painters.

Himalayas and Western China

The Himalayas are the tallest mountains on Earth, yet many people live among them. North of the mountains are the cold, dusty highlands of western China and Mongolia.

Monks and prayer wheels

Tibetan monks

In Tibet, Buddhist monks start their training as young boys. They shave their heads, wear red robes, and join a monastery for life.

The Himalayan peaks are always snowy.

The Himalayas stretch for 2,500 km (1,550 miles).

Mountain villages

In Nepal, villages are dotted about in valleys between the highest mountains. Farmers build flat terraces in the hillsides for growing crops.

Who is the Dalai Lama?

Mongolian horsemen

Mongolians learn to ride by the age of three. Many spend their lives on the move, riding across Mongolia's vast plains with herds of horses and sheep.

Mongolian horse-riding festival

Climbing Everest

The ultimate challenge for a mountaineer is to climb Mount Everest, the world's tallest mountain. Dozens of people reach the summit every year, but some die on the way.

Climbing Mount Everest is exhausting and dangerous.

Buddhist prayer flags

get going
Make Buddhist prayer flags. Attach squares of coloured tissue to a length of string. Hang the string across your room or a garden.

Potala Palace

In the town of Lhasa in Tibet stands a mighty fortress called Potala Palace. It used to be the headquarters of the Tibetan government before Tibet became a part of China.

The useful yak

A yak is kind of huge, shaggy cow that can survive in the cold, thin mountain air. Tibetan people get milk, butter, meat, and wool from yaks.

Basket hangs on back.

Cheese sellers

These Tibetan girls are nomads, which means they move from place to place. They are selling dried yak's cheese.

The head of Tibetan Buddhism and the leader of Tibet's people.

Japan

Japan is made up of four large islands and several thousand small ones. Most of the country is mountainous. The biggest cities are near the coast, where the land is flat.

Snow and ice festival

An ice festival takes place every February in the town of Sapporo. People carve towers of ice into temples, sculptures, or replicas of famous buildings.

Kurile islands

Steller's sea eagle

Hokkaido

Japanese crane

Sapporo

Pollock

Snow monkey

Aomori

Apples

Sushi

Ou Mountains

Cups for rice wine

Honshu

Sea of Japan

N E S W

How many people live in Tokyo?

Robot dog

Ogasawara Islands

Volcano Islands

Toys and gadgets

Japan makes lots of electronic goods, such as computer games, televisions, and robot pets.

Kabuki theatre

Izu Islands

Tokyo

Nagoya Castle

Mount Fuji 3,776 m (12,388 ft)

Nagoya

Pearl in shell

Pacific Ocean

Osaka

Kyoto

Bullet train

Tokyo skyline

The capital city Tokyo is crowded and lively. Its skyscrapers are designed to sway slightly, which protects them from falling during earthquakes.

Oki Islands

Geishas

Chugoku Mountains

Shinto shrine

Hiroshima

Shikoku

Matsuyama castle

Sumo wrestlers

Bonsai tree

Kyushu

Iki

Fukuoka

Nagasaki

Pottery

Sakishima Islands

These small tropical islands lie far to the south of the rest of Japan.

Ishigaki

Iriomote

Yonaguni

Octopus

East China Sea

Ryukyu Islands

Okinawa

Japan

Japan is a fascinating mixture
of old and new. Its people
work very hard and
have made Japan
very wealthy.

Cherry
blossom

Mount Fuji

Mount Fuji

This snow-capped volcano is
the symbol of Japan, and many
Japanese people have a picture
of it in their homes. Mount Fuji
last erupted in 1707.

Snow monkeys

Japanese macaques stay warm in
winter by bathing in hot springs.
These clever monkeys have also
learnt how to make snowballs.

Bullet trains

Japanese "bullet trains"
are among the fastest
trains in the world. They
shoot between cities at
up to 270 kph (167 mph).

Volcano protection

Volcanoes and earthquakes are
common in Japan. In the city of
Kagoshima, children wear helmets
to protect them from rocks and ash
from nearby Mount Sakurajima.

What do Japanese people call their country?

Traditional dress

On special occasions, women and girls wear a kimono – a richly embroidered silk dress tied with a sash.

Cherry blossom

The national flower of Japan is the cherry blossom. In spring, people celebrate the arrival of the cherry blossom with picnics under the trees.

Sumo

Traditional Japanese wrestling is called sumo. The heavy wrestlers try to throw each other out of the ring, called the dohyo.

Thick belt called a mawashi.

Open shoes called zori.

Buddhist temple

Japan's two main religions are Buddhism and Shinto. Buddhist temples, or pagodas, consist of a stack of wooden floors and curved roofs. Ornate gardens often surround them.

Chopsticks

Sushi

Japanese people eat a lot of seafood. Sushi consists of small snacks of rice, raw fish, and vegetables.

Nippon or "the land of the rising Sun."

Australia

Australia is the world's smallest continent, but it is a huge country. Most Australians live on the coast, far from the vast, dusty deserts that make up the outback.

Poisonous animals

More poisonous animals live in Australia than in any other country.

 The male **platypus** has a poisonous spur on each of its back ankles.

A **box jellyfish's** stings can kill and cause terrible pain that lasts for weeks.

 Taipans are the world's deadliest snakes. A bite can kill in 30 minutes.

Sea snake venom can kill a child, but bites from these shy snakes are rare.

 Cone shells are sea snails with deadly stings. The venom causes suffocation.

Funnel-web spiders can bite through a fingernail and stop a person's heart.

 The tiny **blue-ringed octopus** can paralyse and kill a person with its bite.

Darwin

Saltwater crocodile

Boomerang

Broome

Dingo

Tanami Desert

Port Hedland

Great Sandy Desert

Northern Territory

Iron ore

Emu

Road train

Camel

Musgrave

Western Australia

Great Victoria Desert

South Australia

Geraldton

Kalgoorlie

Perth skyline

Perth
Fremantle

Kangaroo

Esperance

Great Australian Bight

Great white shark

Albany

N

W   E

S

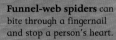

What is a coral reef made from?

Coral reef

The Great Barrier Reef stretches for 2,000 km (1,200 miles) along Queensland's coast. Many brightly coloured fish live on the reef.

Aboriginal paintings

Gulf of Carpentaria

Cape York Peninsula

Cairns

Tennant Creek

The Devils Marbles

Cattle farms

Townsville

Great Barrier Reef

Mount Isa

Mackay

Rainbow lorikeet

Flying doctor

Queensland

Rockhampton

Alice Springs

Simpson Desert

Koala

Uluru (Ayer's Rock)

Sheep stations

Ranges

Pineapple farms

Lake Eyre

Banana plantations

Brisbane

Opals

Coober Pedy

Sydney Opera House

Broken Hill

Funnel-web spider

Port Augusta

New South Wales

Whyalla

Sydney

Wollongong

Kookaburra

Port Lincoln

Adelaide

Wagga Wagga

Murray river

Kangaroo Island

Victoria

CANBERRA

Australian Capital Territory

Mount Gambier

Melbourne

Tram

Bass Strait

Tasmanian devil

Tasmania

Sailing

Hobart

Australia

Australia is on the opposite side of the world from Europe, but most Australians are descended from European settlers. English is the main language in Australia.

Australian shepherds use jeeps to round up their enormous flocks.

Australian Aborigines

The Aborigines have lived in Australia for more than 50,000 years. According to their legends, the world was made by mythical beasts who carved the land into rivers and mountains.

Sheep farms
About a quarter of the world's wool comes from Australia. Some sheep farms are so remote that farmers need planes to visit town.

Boomerangs fly back to you after you throw them.

A boomerang is a throwing weapon that Aborigines use for hunting.

What is the capital of Australia?

Gum trees (eucalyptus trees) have waxy, strong-smelling leaves.

Sydney
Australia's biggest city and chief port is Sydney. Its most famous building is Sydney Opera House in the harbour. Around Sydney are miles of beaches where children can swim and surf after school.

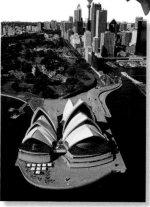

Koala
The only animal that can eat the leaves of Australia's gum trees is the koala. Koalas are very lazy and spend up to 20 hours a day sleeping.

get going
Make an Aboriginal lucky stone. Find a smooth, round pebble and paint a pattern of lines and dots on it to make a picture of an imaginary creature.

On the beach
In Australia, the seasons are the other way round. December is the middle of summer, so Australians celebrate Christmas on the beach.

Bouncing babies
Kangaroos are marsupials — they carry their babies in a pouch. Lots of Australian animals are marsupials.

Kangaroos move by hopping on their huge back feet.

Uluru
Uluru, or Ayers Rock, is a huge lump of sandstone rock in the centre of Australia. Aborigines believe it is a magical place.

New Zealand
and the Pacific

Hundreds of islands are scattered across the Pacific Ocean. Two of the biggest form the mountainous country of New Zealand.

Extreme sports
New Zealand is the world capital for extreme sports. Bungee jumping, sky diving, and white-water rafting are all popular.

Maori war dance
Most people in New Zealand are European, but about one in ten are Maoris – New Zealand's native people. On special occasions, Maoris paint their faces and perform a war dance called a haka.

Moving house
Earthquakes are common in New Zealand, so people live in wooden houses for safety. When people move home, they can carry their house away on a lorry.

Sheep shea▶

Kiwi

South Island

Mount Cook

Christchurch

Takahe

Southern Alps

Rugby

N e w

Queenstown

Dunedin

Bungee jumping

Royal albatross

Sheep

Oysters

116

What's unusual about New Zealand's kiwi birds?

Red snapper

N
W E
S

Auckland

Pohuto geyser

Pacific Ocean

Maori carving   Kiwi fruit

North Island

Parliament buildings (Wellington)

WELLINGTON

Cook Strait

Zealand

Coconut palms
Forests of coconut palms grow along the beaches of the Pacific islands. Islanders climb these tall trees to gather the coconuts.

Pacific islands
About 5 million people live among the tropical islands of the central Pacific.

Northern Mariana Islands (US)

Marshall Islands

Guam (US)

Sperm whale

Palau   Micronesia

Papua New Guinea   Nauru

Solomon Islands   Tuvalu

Kiribati

Tokelau (NZ)

Pacific islanders fish from small wooden canoes.

Vanuatu

Wallis & Futuna (France)   Samoa   American Samoa (US)

Tonga   Niue (NZ)   Cook Islands (NZ)

New Caledonia (France)

Fiji

French Polynesia (France)

Antarctica

The world's coldest continent is
Antarctica, which is covered in
ice. In winter it doubles in size
as the sea freezes around it.

Southern Ocean

Antarctic Peninsula

Weddell Sea

South polar skua

**Halley Research
Station (UK)**

**Ronne Ice
Shelf**

**Ellsworth
Land**

Adélie penguins

Penguins

Lots of sea animals live
around Antarctica's coast.
Penguins are clumsy on land but
superb swimmers underwater.

Krill

Emperor
penguins

NORTH POLE	11,708 MI.
CHRISTCHURCH	2,457 MI.
SEATTLE, WASH.	9,942 MI.
QUONSET PT.	10,538 MI.
ST. PAUL, MINN.	10,002 MI.
SOUTH POLE	831 MI.
SALINAS, CAL.	8,777 MI.
HOUSTON, TEXAS	9,141 MI.
MOBILE, ALA.	9,941 MI.
PONTIAC, MICH.	10,249 MI.

ERECTED BY VX-6 OF 3° WINTERING PARTY 1958
THEY WENT THAT-A-WAY >>

A signpost in Antarctica
shows how far away the
rest of the world is.

Blue whale

Ice-breaker

Scott and the Antarctic

The British explorer Robert Scott
was one of the first people to reach
the South Pole, in 1912. He died of
cold and hunger on the way home.

Antarctic Circle

Southern Ocean

118

Who was the first person to reach the South Pole?

Right whale

Antarctic science

The only people who live in Antarctica are scientists. They use huge balloons to study the climate on Antarctica.

Weather balloon.

Dronning Maud Land

Southern Ocean

Molodezhnaya Station
(Russian Federation)

Survey plane

Adélie penguins

Antarctica

Princess Elizabeth Land

Amundsen-Scott
Station (USA), South
Pole

SOUTH POLE

Snow mobile

Elephant seal

Life in the freezer

Antarctica is so cold that it freezes your breath into icicles around your mouth. People have to cover up in lots of very warm clothes.

Transantarctic Mountains

Vostok Station
(Russian Federation)

Casey Base
(Australia)

Icicles from breath.

Ross Ice Shelf

McMurdo
Air Station (USA)

Ross Sea

Sno-cat

Dumont d'Urville
(France)

Snow petrel

Killer whale

The Norwegian explorer Roald Amundsen, in 1911.

Flags of the World

NORTH AND SOUTH AMERICA

Canada	United States of America	Mexico	Guatemala	Belize	Honduras	El Salvador	Nicaragua
St Kitts and Nevis	Dominica	St Lucia	St Vincent and The Grenadines	Barbados	Grenada	Trinidad and Tobago	Venezuela
Argentina	Paraguay	Uruguay					

AFRICA

			Morocco	Algeria	Tunisia	Libya	Egypt
Guinea-Bissau	Guinea	Sierra Leone	Liberia	Ivory Coast	Burkina	Ghana	Togo
Sao Tome and Principe	Gabon	Congo	Democratic Republic of Congo	Uganda	Rwanda	Burundi	Kenya
Swaziland	South Africa	Lesotho	Madagascar	Comoros	Cape Verde		

EUROPE

						Iceland	Norway
France	Monaco	Germany	Austria	Switzerland	Liechtenstein	Spain	Andorra
Belarus	Ukraine	Moldova	Poland	Czech Republic	Slovakia	Hungary	Slovenia

RUSSIA AND CENTRAL ASIA

Cyprus	Russian Federation	Georgia	Azerbaijan	Armenia	Kazakhstan	Uzbekistan	Turkmenistan
Iraq	Kuwait	Saudi Arabia	Bahrain	Qatar	United Arab Emirates	Oman	Yemen
Vietnam	Cambodia	Philippines	Malaysia	Singapore	Brunei	Indonesia	East Timor

AUSTRALIA AND THE PACIFIC

Maldives	Mauritius	Seychelles	Australia	New Zealand	Palau	Micronesia	Marshall Islands

Which is the only country that doesn't have a rectangular flag?

There are 193 countries in the world. Each has its own flag.

Costa Rica	Panama	Bahamas	Cuba	Jamaica	Haiti	Dominican Republic	Antigua & Barbuda
Colombia	Guyana	Surinam	Ecuador	Peru	Brazil	Bolivia	Chile
Mauritania	Mali	Niger	Chad	Sudan	Eritrea	Senegal	Gambia
Benin	Nigeria	Cameroon	Central African Republic	Ethiopia	Djibouti	Somalia	Equatorial Guinea
Tanzania	Angola	Zambia	Malawi	Mozambique	Namibia	Botswana	Zimbabwe
Sweden	Finland	Denmark	United Kingdom	Ireland	Netherlands	Belgium	Luxembourg
Portugal	Italy	San Marino	Vatican City	Malta	Estonia	Latvia	Lithuania
Croatia	Romania	Bosnia & Herzegovina	Serbia & Montenegro	Bulgaria	Macedonia	Albania	Greece

ASIA

Kyrgyzstan	Tajikistan	Turkey	Iran	Lebanon	Syria	Israel	Jordan
Afghanistan	Pakistan	India	Bangladesh	Sri Lanka	Burma	Laos	Thailand
Papua New Guinea	Mongolia	China	Nepal	Bhutan	North Korea	South Korea	Taiwan	Japan
Nauru	Kiribati	Solomon Islands	Tuvalu	Samoa	Vanuatu	Fiji	Tonga

Index

Reference Section

Acknowledgements

Dorling Kindersley would like to thank:

Andrew O'Brien for additional digital artworks; Chris Bernstein for compiling the index; Lisa Magloff for editorial assistance and proof reading; Abbie Collinson and Sadie Thomas for design assistance; Pilar Morales for DTP assistance; Simon Mumford for DK cartography; Karl Stange, Gemma Woodward, and Sarah Mills for DK Picture Library research

Picture credits